DETAIL Practice

Glass in Building

Principles
Applications
Examples

Bernhard Weller
Kristina Härth
Silke Tasche
Stefan Unnewehr

Birkhäuser
Edition Detail

Authors:
Bernhard Weller, Prof. Dr.-Ing.
Kristina Härth, Dipl.-Ing.
Silke Tasche, Dr.-Ing.
Stefan Unnewehr, Dipl.-Ing. Architect

Project management:
Steffi Lenzen, Dipl.-Ing. Architect

Editorial services:
Nicola Kollmann, Dipl.-Ing. Architect

Editorial assistants:
Melanie Weber, Dipl.-Ing. Architect; Carola Jacob-Ritz, M. A.
Florian Krainer, Dipl.-Ing.; Eva Schönbrunner, Dipl.-Ing.

Drawings:
Dejanira Bitterer, Dipl.-Ing.; Daniel Hajduk, Dipl.-Ing.;
Michal Korte; Simon Kramer, Dipl.-Ing.; Heiko Mattausch, Dipl.-Ing.

Translators (German/English):
Gerd H. Söffker, Philip Thrift, Hannover

© 2009 Institut für internationale
Architektur-Dokumentation GmbH & Co. KG, Munich
An Edition DETAIL book

ISBN: 978-3-0346-0132-0
Printed on acid-free paper made from cellulose bleached without
the use of chlorine.

Typesetting & production:
Simone Soesters

Printed by:
Aumüller Druck, Regensburg
1st edition, 2009

This book is also available in a German language edition
(ISBN 978-3-920034-24-9).

A CIP catalogue record for this book is available from the Library of
Congress, Washington D.C., USA.

Bibliographic information published by Die Deutsche Bibliothek
Die Deutsche Bibliothek lists this publication in the Deutsche
Nationalbibliographie; detailed bibliographic data is available on
the internet at http://dnb.ddb.de.

Institut für internationale
Architektur-Dokumentation GmbH & Co. KG
Hackerbrücke 6, D-80335 München
Telefon: +49/89/38 16 20-0
Telefax: +49/89/39 86 70
www.detail.de

Distribution Partner:
Birkhäuser Verlag AG
PO Box 133, 4010 Basel, Switzerland
Telefon: +41 61 2050707
Telefax: +41 61 2050792
e-mail: sales@birkhauser.ch
www.birkhauser.ch

DETAIL Practice
Glass in Building

Contents

Introduction

Building with glass

This book deals with the use of glass in building as an architectural and engineering discipline. As such, it is concerned with research into the use of glass in the building industry and its deployment in technically complex structures and assemblies that go beyond the knowledge of the glazing trade. The nature and size of these applications call for elaborate methods of calculation or special constructional solutions. In this context, glass is sometimes used not simply as an infill material; instead it is designed to carry loads that exceed the actions per unit area due to self-weight, temperature fluctuations, wind and snow. Such loads result from the diverse tasks that glass has to fulfil besides its usual function as a light-permeable enclosing material. Glass can be used to resist explosions or repel attacks, serve as a safety barrier or trafficable surface, or even function as a loadbearing component in the overall construction. Following descriptions of the basic products, their physical features and the various processing methods (chapter 1), four further chapters explain clearly the principal relationships in the use of glass as a constructional material. The chapter "Glasses for special requirements" is followed by a chapter devoted to architectural design with respect to the optical properties of glass, the particular loadbearing and safety concepts, components and applications ("Designing with glass"). The proper forms of connection, fixing and support are the subject of the next chapter, "Constructing with glass". To enable expeditious, cost-effective and reliable planning, the chapter "Building legislation provisions" provides architects and engineers with everything they need to know about the legal side of building with glass because those applications not covered by rules or regulations may require time-consuming, costly tests. This is followed by a chapter devoted to case studies of structures already built. And finally, the appendix lists standards and sources of further information and includes a glossary to help readers understand the specialised terminology used in this book.

The importance of glass in building

Glass is a fascinating and ambivalent building material. In use, it is, on the one hand, demanding because it does not forgive any design or construction errors, but, on the other hand, indulgent when it is handled properly. When used correctly, its high demands on planning – and often also its high demands on finances – are rewarded by gains in daylight and transparency. Both aspects, i.e. our relationship with the sun and our surroundings, represent elementary human needs that are reflected in the esteem bestowed on this transparent building material. The constantly changing expression of the glass in the play of light and shade evokes stimulating sensual impressions. It is not without reason that the windows of a house are likened to the eyes of a human being.

Production of glass

The production and further development of glass, a man-made material, depends on several factors: the raw materials that form the original mix, the heat energy required to melt those raw materials, the technical conditions of a glassworks or factory, and, last but not least, highly experienced and inventive personnel. The basic composition of the raw materials mix has essentially never altered: sand, potash, or rather soda, and lime. After a method for producing soda artificially was developed in France in the late 18th century, the cost of making glass was cut considerably, which led to soda replacing potash as one of the main constituents. Up until about 1800 the enormous quantity of energy required to raise the tem-

1

perature to the 1500 °C or more necessary to melt the raw materials was achieved almost exclusively with wood. But from the start of the 19th century onwards, coal was increasingly used as the energy source in regions where wood was becoming scarce, e.g. England, and later on the European continent [1].

Up until the end of the 17th century, flat glass could only be produced in a two-stage process that involved producing a hollow vessel first [2]. There were essentially two ways of doing this, which existed side by side owing to the different properties of the resulting glass products: the "blown cylinder sheet glass" and the "crown glass" processes.

In the "blown cylinder sheet glass" process a bulb of glass is blown into a cylindrical vessel with walls of minimum thickness. Once it has cooled, both ends are cut off and the cylinder is slit along its length before it is rolled flat in the flatting furnace. However, the contact with the furnace leaves blemishes on the glass surface.

The "crown glass" process exploits the centrifugal forces that ensue due to fast rotation of a blown glass bulb that is open at one point. Glass produced in this way has a fire-polished surface finish. The smaller pane dimensions possible compared to the blown cylinder sheet glass method were compensated for by the better optical quality of the finished glass product.

But the two methods described above could not satisfy the high demands that large-format mirrors had to meet. In 1688, in the light of this demand, the Frenchman Lucas de Nehou invented the casting and rolling method in which the viscous glass melt is poured onto a metal table and rolled flat [3]. But the subsequent time-consuming grinding and polishing treatment plus a coating turned the cheap

cast glass into an expensive mirror.

Up until that time the raw materials were always heated in batches, but the invention of the continuous tank furnace by Friedrich Siemens in 1867, which he used in his glassworks in Dresden, marks the start of the modern age of glass melt technology [4]. At the start of the 20th century the Belgian Emile Fourcault patented his "drawing method" in which the glass is drawn continuously out of the melt vertically by means of rollers. This method provided the missing piece in the jigsaw of the industrialisation of glass production. As the glass only comes into contact with air, it has a reflective, fire-polished surface finish with a relatively high optical quality. However, the production process often leaves linear distortions in the glass. This flaw was overcome by the Englishman Alastair Pilkington, who in 1959 patented his method that still represents the state of the art in flat glass production – the "float glass method" [5]. In this process the glass melt floats on a bath of liquid tin owing to its lower density and forms a flat layer of glass of constant thickness. The horizontal, endless ribbon of glass leaving the bath of tin is of an extremely high quality (p. 12, Fig. 1).

Architecture and engineering

The development of the use of glass in building has also been affected by progress in other scientific and technical fields. The reason for this can be found in the manufacture and finishing of the glass, but also in the use of this brittle building material in conjunction with other, ductile materials. During the Gothic period, building technology had reached a point where large openings in walls were possible for the first time [6]. A fine network of iron frames formed the supporting construction for the relatively small, often coloured, translucent, diaphanous glass panes.

But the greatest technological advance

was that of the Industrial Revolution. With the aid of the energy sources coal and coke, the steam engine became – literally – the driving force behind an evolution that transformed workshops into factories for producing standardised products in ever greater numbers. This process was speeded up by the fact that many inventions were both the result of and the foundation for industrialisation. Progress in science – especially exact methods for the calculation of loadbearing structures – and political changes, too, e.g. the abolition of a luxury tax on glass in England in 1851, helped to power developments in the building industry. [7]

Initially, it was not the architects who took architecture into the modern age, but rather engineers and planners from so-called non-artistic disciplines [8]. The planning of larger, purely functional, building tasks called for a vision that far exceeded that of the past and solutions whose radical expedience departed from the history of building in both aesthetic and constructional terms. The new forms of construction included sheds over railway stations in which the smoke from the locomotives could disperse, and numerous bridges with spans that had never been seen before. At the same time, the roofs to market halls, shopping arcades and other structures appeared to celebrate the symbiosis of iron and glass.

Whereas in the Gothic age glass helped to achieve the desire for brightness and colour in church interiors, in the early 19th century it was the growing popularity of exotic plants and their need for light and warmth that had a fundamental and lasting effect on architecture. Engineers optimised the building envelopes of many glasshouses, conservatories and orangeries to ensure maximum light transmittance. They were glazed from top to bot-

tom; the shapes of some of them traced the trajectory of the sun across the sky so that the incidence of the sunlight on the glass was always perpendicular. The curved forms with their uniform bending radii represented a sensible compromise between the ideal structural line and the practicalities of industrial prefabrication. Glasshouses not only revolutionised architecture, they also laid the foundation stone for the use of glass as a structural element. For the first time in the history of building, panes of glass were used on a larger scale not only as an infill material but also as a stabilising component. For example, in 1827 John Claudius Loudon reported on his Palm House at Bretton Hall in Yorkshire thus: "When the ironwork was put up, before it was glazed, the slightest wind put the whole of it in motion from the base to the summit … As soon as the glass was put in, however, it was found to become perfectly firm and strong" [9]. Another fundamental concept of the modern use of glass in building was already visible in British glasshouses of that time: the mesh-like glass-and-iron constructions remained stable even if several panes were broken. The fact that many of these structures were not intended to be permanently occupied by people – therefore allowing a lower factor of safety to be assumed – had a positive effect on their design. With their widespread renunciation of historicising applications, great delicacy, overwhelming impression of transparency and use of structurally effective panes of glass (in some instances curved), the aesthetics and construction of glasshouses – in particular the Palm House at the Royal botanic Gardens in Kew near London (Fig. 1) – in some cases even exceeded those of that architectural icon of the 19th century, the Crystal Palace in London, which was designed by Joseph Paxton for the first World Exposition of 1851. At the start of the 20th century the use of

glass in building experienced a new hey-day, especially for industrial and office buildings, which were given large windows and glass facades. This was due to the new manufacturing and finishing methods plus an architectural development we now call the Modern Movement. The next major change came with the oil crisis of the 1970s, which forced the building industry into an energy-efficiency rethink concerning the use of glass products [10]. This resulted in systematic research into building physics relationships and led to the development of special functional glasses. The rising cost of energy together with the increasing awareness of the need for sustainable forms of construction without depleting resources have seen the rise of specialised facades since the 1980s. Their varying, frequently multi-layer constructions, sometimes with controllable functional components, are intended to overcome overheating in summer and reduce energy losses in winter.

Current research is increasingly concerned with hybrid products in which several tasks are combined directly in one component. In the case of facades, for example, experiments are being carried out on curtain walls with glass photovoltaic panels, which can make an active contribution to energy needs, or passive glass loadbearing panel laminates (Figs. 2 and 3). When glass is needed only for the external protective function and transparency is not a requirement, printed or tinted glass is often an option (Fig. 4). The development of light-redirecting glass louvres exploits the optical properties of glass. On a constructional level, research is being carried out into combinations of glass and other, in some cases new, ductile materials, e.g. glass fibre-reinforced plastics. The aim here is to exploit the respective advantages of each material. In addition, plastically shaped glass is being increasingly used

for architectural or structural reasons. The use of suitable adhesives with structural properties – in the automotive industry playing a part in overall stiffness since the 1970s – will also play an ever more significant role in the building industry. Therefore, progress in science and technology today and in the future will permit the design of pioneering glass projects despite ever more stringent safety requirements.

1   A masterpiece of glass-and-iron construction: the Palm House at the Royal Botanic Gardens in Kew near London (GB), 1848, Richard Turner and Decimus Burton
2   Photovoltaic panels in the cavity between the panes of an insulating glass facade (left) and individually controllable glass louvres for redirecting the light (right), Tobias Grau company building, Rellingen (D), 2001, BRT Architekten
3   Test panel of a type of dichroic glass for use as a facade element, e.g. in combination with photovoltaic panels
4   Tinted glass used on the combined police and fire station for the government district in Berlin (D), 2004, sauerbruch hutton architekten

[1]   Glocker, 1992, p. 25ff.
[2]   ibid., p. 76
[3]   ibid., p. 80f.
[4]   ibid., p.16
[5]   ibid., p. 83ff.
[6]   Kohlmeyer, 1998, p. 82
[7]   Glocker, p. 93
[8]   Baum, 2007, p. 185
[9]   Loudon, 1833, p. 980
[10] Glocker, p. 94

Basic glass and derived products

Glass represents a special case among building materials: its transparency enables a different type of construction, which at the same time dictates a different approach because of the particular behaviour of this material. Like a diva among the building materials, glass reacts immediately and sensitively to improper treatment, which has led to its reputation as an unpredictable material. But used properly, it possesses inestimable advantages. And the treatment processes are varied and variable. So we have to know and understand glass as a material.

The material glass
In the scientific sense, the term "glass" refers to a frozen, supercooled liquid that has solidified without crystallisation. It is an amorphous substance produced by melting and rapid cooling, and hence does not have an underlying crystal lattice. This definition allows the term "glass" to stand for a multitude of substances regardless of their chemical composition. For instance, besides natural glasses, e.g. obsidian, metallic glasses or synthetic materials such as acrylic sheet can be allocated to this category.

Generally, when we speak of glass we mean the group of silicate glasses, which account for about 95% of total glass production. These mass-produced glasses consist of about 70% silicon dioxide, i.e. quartz sand, which during the manufacture

of the glass takes on the task of the network former and determines the basic structure of the glass. As quartz sand has a very high melting point (about 1700°C), alkali oxide fluxes are mixed in to lower this. Stabilisers in the form of alkaline earth oxides form another constituent; these are added to improve the hardness and chemical resistance of the glass.

The following are among the most common silicate glasses:
- soda-lime glasses
- lead glasses
- borosilicate glasses

The glasses used in the building industry are in the main of the soda-lime variety. Besides the principal component, silicon dioxide, there is also a proportion of sodium oxide (Na_2O), which in the form of soda acts as a flux. Calcium oxide (CaO) functions as the stabiliser and is dissolved out of the lime that is added to the mix. In addition, there are further constituents in small amounts that depend on the particular raw materials and the processing conditions (Tab. T1). In the case of lead glass, lead oxide (PbO) replaces the calcium oxide. However, with the exception of glass for protection against x-rays, this type of glass has no significance for the building industry. Borosilicate glass – frequently used in the building industry, e.g. for fire-resistant glazing – contains a certain proportion of boron oxide (B_2O_3) instead of calcium oxide. The term alkaline earth glasses refers to a group of glass products which again have silicon dioxide as their main constituent but also contain alkaline earth oxides in varying amounts besides calcium oxide. In these glasses, potassium oxide (K_2O) replaces the sodium oxide. Alkaline earth glasses exhibit a somewhat higher density and a higher modulus of elasticity than soda-lime

glass plus a lower coefficient of thermal expansion. Finally, quartz glass made from pure quartz sand also belongs to the group of silicate glasses, but plays only a minor role.

The properties of glass
Two properties of glass are especially prominent and are firmly tied to this material: its transparency and its fragility.

The transparency is due to the atomic structure, i.e. its non-crystalline nature and the idiosyncrasies of the bonds within the glass itself. The lack of boundary surfaces in the material prevent the reflection of light in the range of visible and long-wave UV-A light; the atomic structure cannot absorb this light, which means that light can pass through unhindered.

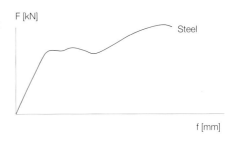

1   Comparison of the mechanical behaviour of steel and glass subjected to tension (F): whereas steel exhibits plasticity after exceeding the elastic limit and is hence highly ductile (f) up until the point of failure, glass exhibits a linear elastic behaviour up to the point of failure, without any plastic material behaviour.

T1: Composition of soda-lime-silica glass to DIN EN 572-1

Silicon dioxide (SiO_2)	69–74 %
Calcium oxide (CaO)	5–14 %
Sodium oxide (Na_2O)	10–6 %
Magnesium oxide (MgO)	0–6 %
Aluminium oxide (Al_2O_3)	0–3 %
Others	0–5 %

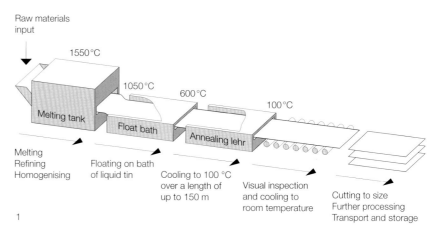

Raw materials input

1550 °C

Melting tank

1050 °C

600 °C

Float bath

Annealing lehr

100 °C

Melting
Refining
Homogenising

Floating on bath of liquid tin

Cooling to 100 °C over a length of up to 150 m

Visual inspection and cooling to room temperature

Cutting to size
Further processing
Transport and storage

1

On the other hand, glass is impermeable to short-wave UV-B and UV-C light because the light energy is sufficient to vibrate the electrons in the glass; this leads to the light being absorbed within the material.

Its fragility and, above all, its sudden failure characterise glass as a typical brittle material. The maximum elongation at failure is in the range of about 0.1 %. Exceeding this elastic deformability by even just a minimal amount results in sudden failure due to rupture without any "waist" forming, together with shell-shaped fracture surfaces. This means that up until this point the glass behaves in an ideal elastic fashion when subjected to mechanical actions. Plastic material behaviour does not occur, which is why it is impossible to predict failure (p. 11, Fig. 1). The high proportion of silicate in the composition of the glass is responsible for this behaviour; however, it is the silicate that gives the glass its hardness and strength. When using glass as a building material it is imperative to consider this fact at all times and to compensate for it through the use of suitable constructional measures (see "Designing with glass", pp. 33–55, and "Constructing with glass", pp. 57–71).

However, when talking about the tensile strength of glass we must distinguish between the theoretical tensile strength (the so-called micro-strength of the glass)

and the practical tensile strength, i.e. the so-called macro-strength. The former, which can be calculated from atomic and ionic bonds in the glass structure, is very high. In the case of pure quartz glass, values between 10 000 and 30 000 N/mm² are possible; in the case of a mixture of raw materials, as is the case with sheet glass, 6500 to 8000 N/mm². In practice, however, sheet glass achieves only a fraction of this theoretical tensile strength. As with all brittle materials, in glass, too, it is the properties of the surface subjected to tension that govern the magnitude of the tensile stresses that can be accommodated. Surface flaws, notches and cracks – mostly invisible to the naked eye – ensue during manufacture and subsequent treatment and handling. When subjected to loads of any kind, stress peaks occur at these defects and the glass cannot accommodate these by way of plastic deformation, which leads to propagation of the cracks. And the longer the load is applied, the greater is the reduction in the load-carrying capacity of the glass. So brief peak loads are less of a problem for glass than lower, long-term loads. As the size of the surface area increases, so does the probability of relevant surface damage occurring at a relatively highly loaded point. So as the size of the area loaded in tension also has an influence on the tensile strength and we cannot predict with any accuracy the occurrence, nature and frequency of any surface defects, the tensile strength can only be designated in the form of a characteristic value for the material. This lies in the range 30–80 N/mm². In contrast to this, the compressive strength reaches very high theoretical values in practice, too. Irrespective of any surface flaws, it lies between 400 and 900 N/mm² for the silicate glasses normally used. As glass is both homogenous and isotropic, these and also all other properties do not depend on direction.

Besides their good surface hardness, silicate glasses also exhibit excellent properties with respect to their resistance to chemicals and are therefore ideal where long-term durability is a requirement. Here again, the silicate basis is the reason for the good corrosion resistance. The majority of acids and alkalis cannot damage glass; one exception, however, is hydrofluoric acid, which is why this acid is used for etching glass surfaces. Glass is also highly resistant to water, but ponding on glass surfaces can lead to leaching in the long-term and hence to corrosion of the glass surface, which manifests itself in the form of cloudy patches. Glass can be damaged by industrial fumes containing ammonia and through contact with plasters/renders, wet concrete or extremely alkaline cleaning agents.

It is primarily the easy mouldability of glass that makes it suitable for use as a building material. Glass has no defined melting point at which sudden liquefying or the onset of melting occurs, as is the case with crystals. Glass is characterised by a continual softening as the temperature rises, which means that upon being heated we observe a constant transition from the brittle material via the viscoelastic range to a viscous melt. It is this property that is exploited for the workability of glass in the form of different production methods plus moulding with the help of heat. The transition range in which glass changes from a brittle to a plastic-viscous material lies between 520 and 550°C for the common, mass-produced silicate glasses.

T2: Properties of soda-lime-silica glass to DIN EN 572-1

Density (at 18 °C)	2500 kg/m³
Modulus of elasticity	70 000 N/mm²
Poisson's ratio	0.2
Average coefficient of thermal expansion	9×10^{-6} K⁻¹
Thermal fatigue resistance	40 K

1   Sketch of the principle of the float glass process
2   Sketch of the principle of the rolled glass process
3   Surface textures of patterned glasses (selection)

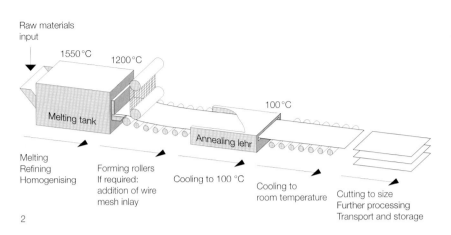

Raw materials input

1550°C 1200°C

Melting tank

100°C

Annealing lehr

Melting
Refining
Homogenising

Forming rollers
If required:
addition of wire
mesh inlay

Cooling to 100 °C

Cooling to
room temperature

Cutting to size
Further processing
Transport and storage

2

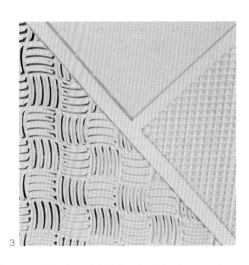

3

Manufacturing the basic products

Sheet glass is the product primarily used for construction applications. All the production methods are preceded by the melting process, the key phase in the manufacture of glass products. The mixture of raw materials trickles into the input end of the melting tank, onto the surface of the glass bath, and melts there to become glass, which is then removed from the other end as a viscous mass and subsequently formed. During this, the three phases take place in certain areas of the tank continuously and simultaneously: the melting of the raw materials takes place at a temperature of about 1550°C; the so-called refining removes any remaining bubbles of gas or air from the molten glass (in order to achieve the desired homogeneity), and, finally, the glass cools down to 1000–1200°C in the subsequent homogenising phase. After that the glass can be worked further.

Float glass
At the start of the 20th century sheet glass was produced by means of a continuous, automated rolling or drawing process that had developed out of the manual methods of the past. When plate glass with a high optical quality was required, the glasses produced by these methods had to be extensively ground and polished afterwards, which was time-consuming and costly. But the float glass method, which was developed by the British Pilkington company between 1952 and 1959 and is now the dominant method in glass manufacture, produced glass with an outstanding surface quality without the need for any additional treatment. This method gradually ousted the other methods of producing sheet glass and today about 35 % of all glass products are manufactured by the float glass method.

In the float process the glass is transferred at a temperature of about 1050°C from the melting tank to the so-called float bath, where it flows as a ribbon of glass on top of liquid tin. This produces sheet glass with parallel faces, flat surfaces and completely undistorted transparency. In the float bath the glass cools down to about 600°C, at which point it has sufficient inherent strength to be lifted from the tin bath and transported into the annealing lehr to cool further. Following cooling, the subsequent working can begin (Fig. 1).

The glass thicknesses possible with this method lie in the range 0.5–25 mm, but for practical building purposes thicknesses between 2 and 19 mm are typical. The normal conditions during the float process cause a so-called equilibrium thickness of approx. 7 mm to become established automatically. Adjusting the top rollers – serrated wheels resting on the edges of the ribbon of glass at the front end of the float bath – enable the production of thinner and thicker glasses. However, thicknesses > 12 mm are not readily possible because these cannot be achieved with the top rollers alone and additional, non-wetted longitudinal guides (so-called fenders) have to be installed. These lateral limits enable a thicker ribbon of glass to be formed. The manufacturing process itself results in the two sides of the glass having different chemical compositions. The side in contact with the liquid tin – the bath side – has a higher content of tin ions than the so-called air side. This difference is invisible but can lead to varying behaviour during subsequent processes. Float glass to DIN EN 572-2 must exhibit a characteristic tensile bending strength of 45 N/mm². The permissible tensile bending strengths used in design depend on the type of application and must be taken from the relevant code of

practice (see "Building legislation provisions", pp. 73–81).

Rolled glass
This is sometimes called cast glass, a name that stems from the earlier method of manufacture in which the molten glass was poured onto a flat table and subsequently rolled flat. The modern production of rolled glass involves passing a continuous ribbon of glass, which leaves the melting tank as a viscous glass mass at a temperature of about 1200 °C, between two water-cooled, contra-rotating rollers. The gap between the two rollers, one above the other, can be adjusted to control the thickness of the ribbon of glass, which can lie between 3 and 15 mm. After that, the glass is transported on rollers into the annealing lehr before being subsequently cut to size (Fig. 2). The standard dimensions available depend on the manufacturer and the specific rolled glass product required. The light permeability of rolled glass is inferior to that of float glass and depends on thickness and surface texture.

Rolled glass is used for various products. Patterned glass, which is available in various designs, is produced by using a textured lower roller (Fig. 3). Wired glass, with or without a patterned surface, is manufactured by introducing a wire mesh prior to rolling (Fig. 2). Polished wired glass is obtained through subsequent grinding and polishing. The characteristic tensile bending strength of these glass products must be 25 N/mm².

Profiled glass (also known as channel glass) is also produced from rolled glass. The edges of narrow rolled ribbons of glass are turned up through 90° by vertical rollers to create a U-shaped section (Fig. 1 and Tab. T3). This glass can also be produced with textured surfaces or a wire mesh inlay. As these products can

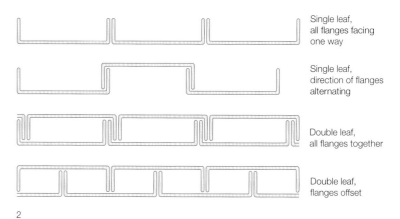

Single leaf,
all flanges facing
one way

Single leaf,
direction of flanges
alternating

Double leaf,
all flanges together

Double leaf,
flanges offset

2

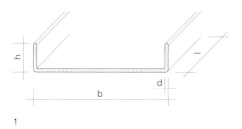

1

T3: Dimensions of profiled glass to DIN EN 572-7 (see Fig. 1)

Thickness (d)	6 mm, 7 mm
Length (l)	250–7000 mm
Width (b)	232–498 mm
Flange width (h)	41 mm, 60 mm

carry high loads because of their cross-sectional form, they are ideal for use without glazing bars, or as single- or double-leaf constructions when inserted into peripheral lightweight metal frames (Fig. 2). The thermal performance can be improved by placing transparent thermal insulation between the flanges.

Drawn glass
The various drawing methods cannot compete with the float process in terms of productivity and quality. This type of glass therefore plays a only a subsidiary role in the building industry. In the method used today, the continuous ribbon of glass is drawn vertically out of the melt. This drawing process leaves the glass with a less than optimal optical quality, as is often encountered in historical glasses. Drawn glass is therefore often used for restoration projects on old buildings, with some surface flaws deliberately introduced, and is often marketed under brand-names such as "antique". Depending on the type of sheet glass, lengths between 1.20 and 2.16 m and widths between 1.45 and 2.88 m are available. Thicknesses range from 2 to 12 mm.

Colourless, tinted and opal glass
Soda-lime glasses with typical compositions (Tab. T1) have a slight greenish tint, which is primarily evident at the edges. This is caused by the proportion of iron oxide in the sand used. True colourless glass, known as extra-clear or low-iron glass, is produced by using a mix with an especially low proportion of iron oxide. The iron oxide is almost totally removed by a chemical process.
All sheet glass basic products can also be tinted. This is achieved by mixing various metal oxides into the melting tank or through a subsequent colouring process. The latter method is particularly useful when only small quantities are required.

Adding colour can also have an effect on physical properties of the glass such as light transmission.
Opal glass is produced by adding fluorine compounds, phosphates or tin oxide. The glass obtained is light-permeable, but no longer transparent. Such glass can also be tinted.

Sheet glass treatments
The sheet glass basic products mentioned above, particularly float glass with its high optical quality, represent the starting point for further treatment. The forms of subsequent treatment possible are carried out in several stages and are aimed at modifying the glass for functional reasons as well as achieving purely decorative changes.

Mechanical working
Cutting to size is the first process that the newly produced sheet glass undergoes. Float glass is generally cut to the international ribbon size of 3.21 × 6.0 m. The width of 3.21 m is determined by the width of the float glass plant, the length of 6.0 m is primarily determined by transport and further processing requirements. Lengths up to 8.0 m are possible (Fig. 3), but such lengths represent custom-made components that can well involve higher costs. The sizes of the other basic products cannot match those of float glass. The glasses available in ribbon or standard dimensions can be subsequently cut to the most diverse shapes and sizes depending on requirements and applications. Glass is normally cut by means of scoring and then snapping the material, less frequently with the help of diamond-tipped saws or water jets. Very thin glasses can also be cut with lasers.

As cutting the glass represents an intervention in the surface of the edge and hence damage to that surface, subse-

3

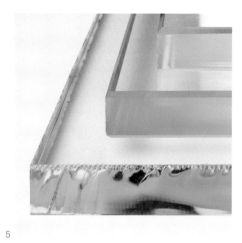

4   Section   Elevation   5

Edge left as cut

Chamfered arrises, edge not ground

Chamfered arrises plus ground edge

Polished edge

quent working of the edge is necessary for almost all applications (Figs. 4 and 5). This is necessary in order to eliminate the irregularities caused by the cutting, which would otherwise cause the tensile strength in this zone to be considerably reduced. Edges may be simply left as cut, but they can be ground and polished as well. They can be ground to a certain profile with diamond-tipped multi-grit tools. Edges that are ground to the required pane dimensions but still exhibit flaws in the edge surfaces are designated as "ground to size". Some manufacturers no longer offer this grade, but only the ground edge as the next higher level of quality. This edge exhibits a distinctly matt satin appearance without any flaws. Subsequent polishing of the ground edges produces transparent edges again, and this represents the highest edge quality. Various kinds of profiled edges plus rounded and chamfered arrises are possible, in addition to straight edges.

Drilled holes and cutouts in the glass, e.g. for point fixings at a later date, are produced with diamond-tipped hollow drills, working from both sides, or with water jets. The latter method in particular means that all manner of shapes and contours are possible. Both cylindrical and tapered holes can be cut for attaching point fixings (see "Constructing with glass", pp. 64–67). The arrises to these drilled holes should also be worked because just like cut edges they represent a weakness in the pane of glass. And as these fixings are points of load transfer, they are subjected to especially high stresses.

Surface treatments
The surface of the glass can be modified by various means. The treatment can in turn influence a series of properties of the glass, create new functions or achieve artistic effects.

Coating the glass with a thin film of metal or metal oxide plays an important role here. These coatings normally consist of systems with several individual layers and are either applied to the surface of the glass during the manufacturing process, i.e. while the surface is still fluid (online method), or afterwards, once the sheet glass has been produced (offline method). The online method produces a very strong and durable bond between the glass and the coating, which results in a hardwearing surface not vulnerable to scratches or other damage. On the other hand, the coatings applied in the offline method are frequently less resistant to environmental influences and mechanical actions. When such surfaces are very vulnerable, these must be placed on the inside of multi-pane insulating or laminated glass products to protect them from atmospheric effects. The mechanical properties of the glasses are not influenced by the ultra-thin coatings. Typical applications include solar-control and low E glasses. The former are given metallic coatings that enable a high reflection capacity in the infrared range, for example. Nevertheless, a high transmission capacity in the range of visible light is still a requirement. Good sunshading is, however, always linked with a reduction in the light transmission. These glasses can be obtained in a range of tints extending from colourless to greenish, bluish or greyish. Glasses with anti-reflection coatings exhibit greater transparency. The coating reduces the reflection from the normal value of about 8 % to a residual reflection of about 1 %, thus increasing the light transmission. The opposite case of increased reflection is also possible. To achieve colour effects, glasses can be provided with so-called dichroic coatings. These combine layers of high and low refraction to create impressions of changing colours on a facade, varying with the angle of incidence

of the light, viewing angle and background. Glasses can be provided with dirt-repellent surfaces to reduce soiling and ease cleaning (self-cleaning glass). Switchable electrochromic coatings allow the optical properties of the glass to be controlled and hence, for example, the solar radiation permeability to be regulated as required. Whether the glass can be further processed, e.g. thermally toughened or bent, depends on the type of coating.

So-called enamelled glasses are actually treated with ceramic inks. These are thick-film coatings applied to the whole surface on one side of the glass by rolling or casting (p. 16, Fig. 1), or just to certain areas to create particular patterns or pictures by way of silk-screen printing (p. 16, Fig. 3). The ceramic ink is baked into the glass surface at a very high temperature (within the scope of thermal toughening) and thus creates a weather-resistant surface. Besides the decorative change to the surface, e.g. for spandrel panels, a pane with silk-screen printing can also be used to create a non-slip surface useful for trafficable glass. Enamelled glass can appear opaque, translucent or transparent, depending on the colours chosen, glass thickness and viewing angle. It should be realised that the enamelling reduces the tensile strength of the glass surface treated.
Painting glass without subsequent stove-enamelling is used for internal applications only.

1   Dimensions of profiled glass (see Tab. T3)
2   Examples of the use of profiled glass components
3   Example of the installation of float glass panes 8 m long, or rather high (bespoke production)
4   Schematic diagrams of edge forms
5   Float glass with edge left as cut (bottom), ground edge (middle) and polished edge (top)

1

2

3

Whereas coating and enamelling represent "additive" methods that create a new surface outside the glass matrix, in "subtractive" methods the defined removal of material creates a new surface within the glass matrix. The two customary methods for this latter process are sand-blasting and etching the glass with hydrofluoric acid. Both these methods can be applied to the whole surface of the glass or just certain areas, and in different intensities. So-called frosted or obscured glass is roughened to the same degree over its entire surface so that the light is scattered diffusely. It is primarily etching that enables a very homogenous surface with a velvety texture and reproducible quality to be produced, combining transparency with opacity (Fig. 2).

Bent glass
Bent, or curved, glass is produced by shaping the basic product at a temperature of about 600 °C. This is carried out either in horizontal roller-type bending plants or, in the case of smaller batches, using the gravity bending method in which the flat pane of glass is laid over a convex or concave "mould" and then heated. The force of gravity causes the glass to take on the shape of its mould. All manner of bent forms are feasible: cylindrical shapes, with or without straight extensions, spherical, conical or parabolic shapes (Fig. 4), even S-profiles. The limits for bending glasses – in terms of maximum bending angle, minimum radii and maximum dimensions – vary according to manufacturer. As the bending technology is being continuously developed, even the maximum float glass pane size (3.21 × 6.0 m) can now be bent. However, the maximum size does depend on the final product that is to be manufactured:
· thermally toughened glass
· laminated safety glass
· multi-pane insulating glass

Basic products for bent glass are:
· clear or tinted float glass
· coated and silk-screen printed glasses
· patterned glasses
· wired or patterned wired glass

Thermally toughened glass
The special optical properties of glass, its good hardness, light-fastness, thermal stability and resistance to radiation and chemicals all give it a good reputation as a building material. The disadvantages, however, are its low tensile strength, dependent on the surface properties, and its brittle fracture behaviour, with the associated high risk of injuries. The thermal toughening process plays an important role in compensating for these weaknesses. The principle is similar to that of prestressed concrete: in order to be able to accommodate higher tensile stresses without damage, the glass is "overcompressed" in such a way that the inherent compressive strength must be overcome first before a tensile stress can build up in the glass. In contrast to prestressed concrete, however, in which this prestress is introduced from outside during the construction process, the prestress in the glass is introduced in the factory after the glass has been manufactured. The glass to be toughened is first heated up to a temperature of 620–650°C. This temperature is far higher than the transformation temperature of glass at which the properties of the brittle, solid material are lost and the behaviour of a viscous material becomes evident. The heating is followed by an abrupt cooling process – jets of air applied to both sides of the glass to restore it to room temperature. During this cooling process the surfaces of the glass cool and solidify first, before the inner core hardens. As the temperature drops further, the surfaces – already solid – are placed in a state of compression as a result of the thermal contraction of the

inner core. The compressive stresses are in equilibrium with the tensile stresses – caused by the heat – within the pane of glass (Figs. 6a and 6b). Consequently, the toughening process results in an equilibrium stress state without the application of any external loads (inherent stress state). Besides a higher tensile bending strength due to the compressive stress that has been introduced into the surfaces, thermally toughened glass exhibits thermal fatigue and impact resistances that are far higher than those of float glass. All sheet glass products (without a wire inlay) can be used as the basic material for producing thermally toughened glass, but also bent and even coated glasses, provided the type of coating permits this. Enamelled glass is always toughened because thermal treatment is necessary for applying the ceramic inks. However, it is not possible to achieve a flatness equal to that of glass cooled in the normal way, i.e. minor distortions can occur. All mechanical operations, e.g. cutting, drilling and edge working, must be completed before carrying out the heat treatment because otherwise the inherent stresses in the glass would cause the glass to fracture during such processes. Edge working in advance minimises the risk of breakage during the toughening process itself. We distinguish between two types of thermally enhanced glass: toughened safety glass and heat-strengthened glass.

1   The curved enclosure to the hall is glazed with panes coated with ceramic inks and is lit from behind at night; Festival Hall, St. Polten (A), 1997, Klaus Kada
2   Facade of etched, matt glass; art gallery, Bregenz (A), 1997, Peter Zumthor
3   The artistic design of the facade was achieved with silk-screen printing; Ramsar visitors centre, Schrems (A), 2006, ah3 Architekten

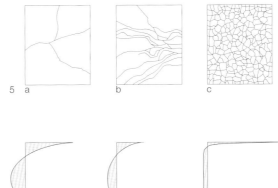

5 a   b   c

6 a   b   c

Due to the toughening process, toughened safety glass exhibits compressive stresses in the surface in the order of magnitude of about 100–150 N/mm². The high energy stored in this inherent stress state means that upon fracture the glass shatters into a shower of small blunt-edged dice, with the fineness of the fracture pattern increasing with the degree of prestress (Fig. 5c). The risk of a broken pane of glass causing injuries is thus considerably reduced. Besides the positive aspect of the better strength and the reduced risk of injuries, it is still important to realise that a pane of toughened safety glass loses its load-bearing capacity totally and immediately upon breakage, and that the fragments of broken glass can become interlocked to such an extent that they do not break into small dice until after impact. Toughened safety glass alone therefore cannot satisfy the safety requirements in every situation. It is produced in thicknesses from 3 to 25 mm. The maximum and minimum dimensions depend on the respective manufacturer, but toughening float glass with the absolute maximum (non-standard) pane dimensions possible at present (3.21 × 8.0 m) is already feasible. Toughened safety glass to DIN EN 12150-1 exhibits a thermal fatigue resistance of 200 K and when using float glass as the basic product a characteristic tensile bending strength of 120 N/mm². When using enamelled glass or other basic products made from soda-lime-silica glass, lower strength values are to be expected.

Invisible nickel sulphide (NiS) inclusions in toughened safety glass, which are the result of unavoidable impurities in the glass mix, can lead to spontaneous fracture of toughened safety glass panes. The reason for this is the increase in volume of the particles which occurs over time due to a phase change. In addition, nickel sul-

phide exhibits a higher coefficient of thermal expansion than that of glass, which can increase the risk of the pane shattering as it gets warmer, e.g. when exposed to sunlight. Additional heating of the panes for eight hours at a temperature of about 290 °C (heat-soak test) can reduce this risk considerably. This additional heating accelerates the crystallisation of the nickel sulphide particles to such an extent that any panes with inclusions break at this point. Panes of glass that pass the heat-soak test undamaged are designated as heat-soaked toughened safety glass.

Heat-strengthened glass undergoes the same manufacturing process as toughened safety glass except that the cooling process is slower. This results in a lower inherent compressive stress in the surfaces than is the case with toughened safety glass and hence a tensile bending strength that although higher than that of float glass is below that of toughened safety glass. DIN EN 1863 specifies a characteristic value of 70 N/mm² for heat-strengthened glass made from float glass. The thermal fatigue resistance is also lower than that of toughened safety glass, but at 100 K is still higher than that of float glass. One great difference between toughened safety and heat-strengthened glass is the fracture pattern of the latter, the coarse structure of which is similar to that of float glass (Fig. 5b). Consequently, it is not possible to reduce the risk of injuries. The decisive advantage of heat-strengthened glass, however, is its suitability for further processing to form laminated safety glass: the coarse fracture pattern lends it a certain residual load-bearing capacity in the event of breakage which cannot be achieved by laminated safety glass made from toughened safety glass. As the slow cooling process becomes harder to control as the panes become thicker, heat-strengthened glass

is generally only produced in thicknesses up to 12 mm. Once again, the maximum and minimum dimensions depend on the manufacturer. Spontaneous breakages due to nickel sulphide inclusions are a rarity with heat-strengthened glass, which is apparently due to the slower cooling process or the lower tensile stresses in the inner core.

Chemically toughened glass
Glass that has been chemically toughened plays only a subsidiary role in the building industry and is primarily used for very thin panes and complicated three-dimensional geometries. Exchanging the ions in the surface for ions having a larger atomic radius causes an increase in volume. The material deeper within the pane attempts to resist the enlargement and generates a compressive stress at the surface. The stresses are higher than is the case with thermally toughened glass, but they extend only a very short distance into the material (Fig. 6c). The fracture pattern is similar to that of float glass and subsequent working is possible to a limited extent only. Chemically toughened glass is primarily used for optical applications and in the automotive industry.

4 Use of insulating glass bent to a tapered shape for the entrance lobby to an office building; 10 Gresham Street, London (GB), 2003, Foster + Partners
5 Schematic presentations (not to scale) of the fracture patterns of untreated and thermally toughened glasses
   a Float glass
   b Heat-strengthened glass
   c Toughened safety glass
6 Stress distribution over the thickness of a toughened glass pane. Near the surface the glass is in compression, in the middle in tension. The exact stress distribution varies depending on the toughening process.
   a Toughened safety glass
   b Heat-strengthened glass
   c Chemically toughened glass

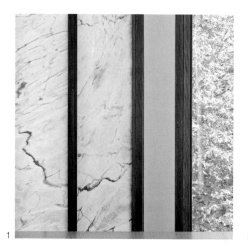

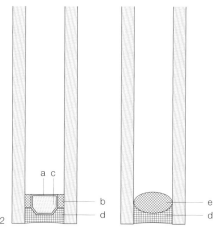

Laminated glass and laminated safety glass
Even toughened glass cannot satisfy all the safety requirements of the construction industry. The possibility of failure without any loadbearing reserves prohibits the use of single panes as loadbearing elements in structural applications in building. This problem can be overcome by bonding two or more sheets of glass by means of viscoelastic interlayers.

The safety requirements that have to be satisfied by laminated safety glass are very precisely defined: in the event of the pane of glass breaking, the elastic interlayer has to hold together the fragments, limit the size of any opening caused by the breakage and hence ensure enhanced protection against injuries caused by fragments or splinters of glass; in addition, once broken, the pane must also exhibit a certain residual load-bearing capacity (in combination with the supporting construction). This latter feature is especially important in overhead applications. Laminated safety glass therefore has a decisive advantage over toughened safety glass, which collapses completely once broken: the space-enclosing function of the former remains essentially intact and it still provides adequate protection even though severely damaged. Generally, laminated safety glass is produced with an interlayer of polyvinyl butyral (PVB film) because this material exhibits optimum mechanical properties for this type of usage plus high tear elongation and tear strength. In addition, it has good light-fastness and outstanding optical properties, which ensure undistorted transparency. A pane of laminated safety glass consists of at least two panes of glass bonded together with a PVB film just 0.38 mm thick, or a multiple of this depending on the requirements. However, depending on the application, it is also possible to bond together several panes and interlayers to form a multi-ply element. All sheet glass basic products

can be used, but also toughened glass, bent glass or glasses with a surface treatment. Translucent or opaque interlayers, also those with various tints or patterns, are available in addition to the transparent, colourless variety. In the case of tinted interlayers, it is advisable to use toughened glasses because the increased absorption of sunlight heats up the glass to a greater extent and increases the risk of heat-induced breakage. The lamination of sheet glass products is generally carried out in a two-stage operation. After laying the film between the two panes of glass to be bonded, a preliminary bond is generated by rolling at a temperature of 70°C. The adhesive bond is completed in an autoclave at pressures > 10 bar and temperatures a little over 100°C. During this process any residual air in the laminated product is dissolved, thus producing a stable unit with undistorted transparency. Laminated safety glass is produced in sizes up to 3.21 x 6.0 m, and lengths up to 8.0 m are even possible. Anti-vandal, anti-intruder, bullet-resistant and blast-resistant glasses are special forms of laminated safety glass with multiple layers or modified configurations (see "Glasses for special requirements", pp. 24–25).

Laminated glass merely has to guarantee a permanent bond between the glasses over the whole area. This designation includes all multi-ply glazing units with other forms of interlayer. The following are examples of interlayer materials:
· Reaction resins in a thickness of 1–4 mm, mainly used for sound insulating glasses
· Other types of thermoplastic films, e.g. ethylene vinyl acetate (EVA), which are very popular for embedding photovoltaic modules in glasses
· Gel interlayers for multi-ply fire-resistant glazing
· Textile inlays or PE sheets printed with

pictures between two layers of PVB film, for decorative purposes

One special type of planar bond is the joining of glass to stone slabs just a few millimetres thick by means of a transparent sheet, which results in interesting optical effects (Fig. 1).

Multi-pane insulating glass
Another method of joining glasses is seen in the production of multi-pane insulating glass. Here, at least two panes of glass are joined together by way of a shear-resistant connection along their perimeters, which creates a hermetically sealed cavity filled with air or a gas. This measure improves the thermal insulation considerably over that of an individual pane. With a cavity just 12 mm wide, no special infill gas and uncoated glasses, the thermal transmittance (U-value) compared to a monolithic pane is reduced by half. The width of the cavity can be between 4 and 24 mm; cavities between 12 and 20 mm are typical these days. Various, also modified, sheet glass products can be used, with identical or different thicknesses, flat or curved, or with the most diverse geometries.

The edge seal commonly in use these days is in the form of a metal (steel, aluminium), approximately rectangular spacer bar, which sets the width of the cavity, and a two-stage organic sealing system that bonds and seals (Fig. 2). The inner seal is generally made from polyisobutylene (butyl), which has only a low adhesion and in the first place is intended to prevent water vapour diffusion and thus avoid condensation between the panes. The outer seal is of polysulphide, polyurethane or silicone and ensures a firm connection plus additional sealing. Of these secondary sealing materials, however, only silicone has good UV resist-

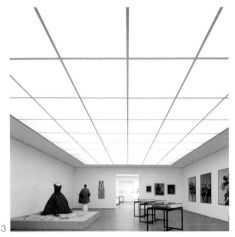

ance, which means that when the other materials are used, the edges must be protected against solar radiation. In order to prevent small amounts of moisture (possibly introduced during the production process or infiltrating at a later date) condensing on the inside of the panes, the metal spacer contains a desiccant. If the cavity between the glasses is filled with a noble gas (argon, krypton, xenon) to improve the thermal or sound insulation, the edge seal must also prevent any loss of the gas. Silicone is unsuitable as a secondary sealing material in this case because it exhibits a relatively high diffusion rate for such types of infill gas. As an alternative, the edge seal can make use of a two-stage, organic sealing system without a metal spacer, which always represents a weak spot in the thermal insulation anyway (TPS = Thermo Plast Spacer, Fig. 2). The desiccant for absorbing any infiltrating moisture is forced into the inner seal of butyl compound. The second, outer seal is again made from a conventional insulating glass sealant.

Bowing and dishing of the panes of a multi-pane insulating unit once installed can lead to optical distortions. The reason for such deformations are the different pressures between and outside the panes, which are due to changes in the air pressure, temperature and altitude between place of manufacture and place of installation. This fact must be taken into account when designing multi-pane insulating units.

Multi-pane insulating units are primarily used for low E and solar-control glass elements, but also for sound insulating glass units (see "Glasses for special requirements", pp. 21–23 and 29–31). The possibility of including fixed or movable functional layers in the cavity (sunshades, anti-glare screens, light-scattering/redirecting elements) renders possible a multitude of

functional glasses which can be optimised in terms of their building physics and architectural requirements. As with all the other glass products, the dimensions of multi-pane insulating units depend on the manufacturer, but custom sizes up to 3.21 × 8.0 m are already possible.

Further glass products
Besides the aforementioned types of glass there are also many other products that are used only occasionally in glass constructions. It is difficult to compile an exhaustive list, the following types represent a few examples.

Flashed glass
Flashed glass is a drawn sheet glass product that consists of a transparent basic glass plus a layer of opal or tinted glass; the two are fused together in the production process. This type of glass in its opaque-white variant is used, for example, in ceilings and walls lit from behind to ensure even room illumination without glare (Fig. 3).

Fusing glass
This is made from glasses of different colours fused together at a temperature of about 790–900°C to create a translucent, textured, coloured material. Fusing glass can be further processed to form toughened or multi-pane insulating glass.

Glass blocks
Glass blocks (or glass bricks) are pressed glass products made by fusing together two open half-blocks to create an airtight hollow unit. They are translucent, can be tinted, are available with smooth or textured surfaces and are used for walls (Fig. 4).
Glass ceramics
Strictly speaking, glass ceramics do not belong to the group of glass types because the crystal growth in the melt so undesirable for glass products is in this case pro-

moted during the production. These products can be produced in various colours and in transparent, translucent or opaque versions. In everyday use, glass ceramics are used for cooker hobs, and in the building industry as cladding for facades.

1 Stone-and-glass composite facade construction; library of the University of Applied Sciences, Dresden (D), 2006, ReimarHerbst.Architekten
2 Vertical sections through typical edge seals for multi-pane insulating glass units with metal spacer (left) and without metal spacer (right)
  a Metal spacer
  b Inner seal
  c Desiccant
  d Outer seal
  e Inner seal with integral desiccant
3 Lighting ceiling with opaque-white flashed glass; Hamburger Bahnhof Museum, Berlin (D), 1997, Kleihues + Kleihues
4 Close-up of facade corner built with glass blocks of different sizes (internal); Maison Hermes, Tokyo (J), 2001, Renzo Piano Building Workshop

When used as an enclosing element within the building envelope, the tasks of glass are to allow daylight into the interior and to provide adequate protection from the weather. The transparency of glass enables both requirements to be combined. Furthermore, glass is also being used increasingly for loadbearing functions in the building structure and envelope, and in the scope of such applications must also satisfy more and more building physics demands. This chapter explains how, through suitable constructions and choice of materials plus additional coatings, derived glass products can be used to meet thermal insulation, solar-control, sound insulation, fire protection and safety/security requirements.

Sound insulation

Through their sense of hearing, human beings perceive mechanical vibrations that propagate in gases, liquids and solids and are then transmitted to the ears in the form of airborne sound. The audible frequencies lie in the range of about 16 to 20 000 vibrations per second, which are specified in Hertz (Hz) and determine the pitch perceived by the listener. The audible range of loudness covers an extremely high range of sound pressures amounting to about six powers of 10. The perception of loudness depends not only on the sound pressure, but also on the frequency: a high frequency is perceived as louder than a low frequency with the same sound pressure. Noise is the sound we perceive as annoying or disturbing.

It is the task of passive noise control to protect people in enclosed rooms against unreasonable annoyances caused by sound transmissions. Passive noise control comprises all measures that serve to reduce the sounds, i.e. improve the sound insulation. Reducing the noise from outside a building is particularly relevant in this respect.

The sound reduction index R and the weighted sound reduction index R_w are used to assess the degree of sound insulation.

The sound reduction index R describes the relationship between the incident sound intensity and the emitted sound power in the form of a function related to the building component. The building acoustics measurements required for this according to DIN EN 20140 relate to the frequency range between 100 and 3150 Hz because studies have revealed that it is only this range that is relevant. The index R designates the airborne sound insulation of building components in test setups without flanking transmissions. The modified index R' takes into account the sound transmission via adjoining components which is unavoidable in reality. Halving the sound pressure corresponds to an 10 dB improvement in the sound insulation. The true noise level in the interior is influenced by the finishes, furnishings and fittings and also the size of the room. Typical office interiors help to reduce the noise by about 3–5 dB.

The level of sound insulation is specified by the weighted sound reduction index R_w or R'_w as a single figure in order to simplify the formulation of minimum requirements and ease the comparison of different building components. The calculation of R_w is carried out iteratively according to DIN EN ISO 717 using a standardised reference curve that enables an assessment relevant to the human ear. This is shifted by whole decibels with respect to the true sound insulation curve R, resulting in both higher and lower values. The differences between the curves are read off and added together for 16 specified frequencies. The sum of the unfavourable deviations divided by the number of measurements (16) should be as large as possible, but no greater than two. Taking into account the

human perception of loudness, R_w is read off the shifted reference curve at a frequency of 500 Hz. DIN 4109 stipulates the sound insulation requirements that building components have to satisfy in the form of minimum required sound reduction indexes (reqd. R'_w). Proof of compliance must be provided by calculation or measurements.

Assessing the sound insulation effect solely according to the weighted sound reduction index R_w is suitable for solid components, but not for glass. In the case of multi-pane insulating glass in particular, the level of sound insulation drops in the frequency range relevant for building acoustics because of the cavity between the panes. This means it is possible that two glazing systems with an identical weighted sound reduction index R_w may insulate against noise very differently in certain frequency ranges (Fig. 1). In order to take this fact into account, spectrum adaptation terms C and C_{tr} have been determined from the measurement curve of the glass according to DIN EN ISO 717.

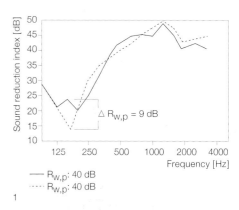

1   Sound insulation curves of two acoustic glazing units with different sound insulation properties in certain frequency ranges but the same weighted sound insulation index (determined under test conditions)

T1: Spectrum adaptation terms C and C_{tr} depending on source of noise according to DIN EN ISO 717-1

Source of noise	Spectrum adaptation term
Dwelling activities (conversation, music, radio, TV) Children playing Medium- and high-speed rail traffic Motorway traffic > 80 km/h Jet aircraft at close range Operations emitting primarily medium- and high-frequency noise	C
Urban road traffic Low-speed rail traffic Propeller aircraft Distant jet aircraft Disco music Operations emitting primarily low- and medium-frequency noise	C_{tr}

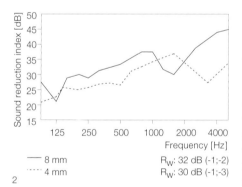

— ·— Noise spectrum 1 (slow road traffic)
········ Noise spectrum 2 (fast road traffic/aircraft)
——— Sound insulation curve of window

1

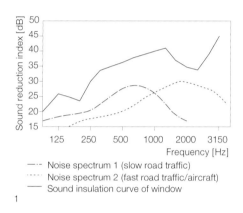

| ——— 8 mm | R_W: 32 dB (-1;-2) |
| ········ 4 mm | R_W: 30 dB (-1;-3) |

2

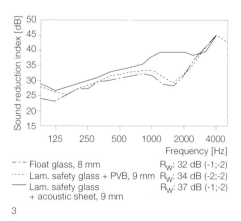

— —— Float glass, 8 mm	R_W: 32 dB (-1;-2)
········ Lam. safety glass + PVB, 9 mm	R_W: 34 dB (-2;-2)
——— Lam. safety glass + acoustic sheet, 9 mm	R_W: 37 dB (-1;-2)

3

These factors can be used to represent the true level of sound insulation. They therefore represent a measure of the inconstancy ranges in the sound insulation curves for glazing.

Figs. 1 and 2 show that the sound insulation curve drops in the upper and lower frequency ranges. The spectrum adaptation term C_{tr} takes into account the lower frequency ranges, e.g. environmental noise due to road traffic, slow rail traffic or distant aircraft. The spectrum adaptation term C covers high frequency ranges, e.g. due to fast road and rail traffic, nearby aircraft or children playing (Tab. T1). These factors are almost always negative or zero. They indicate by how many decibels the weighted sound reduction index R_w must be corrected. The value R_w is then specified in dB in the form $R_w(C; C_{tr})$. If, for example, R_w according to EN ISO 717-1 is specified as $R_w(C; C_{tr}) = 37(-1; -3)$, then the actual sound reduction index in the higher frequency range is only 36 dB, and for noise due to road traffic the weighted sound reduction index must be reduced by 3 dB, to 34 dB. This approach means that the level of sound insulation of acoustic glazing can be assessed realistically and not, as was common in the past, overestimated.

Sound pressure fluctuations can vibrate solid building components to only a limited extent. In principle we can say that the heavier a component, the greater its sound insulating effect. Glass in a facade therefore represents a weak spot because of its comparatively low weight per unit area. Nevertheless, by using suitable types of glazing, sound reduction indexes > 50 dB are feasible. Such glazing should consist of two or more panes of glass with a casting resin interlayer or special acoustic sheets. One- or two-part casting resin systems can be used; the

one-part systems cure through the action of UV light. The sound insulating function is based on the elasticity of the resin, which can be tuned to certain frequency ranges and can attenuate the internal vibrations.

A monolithic pane of glass behaves almost identically to a pane of laminated safety glass of the same thickness over the frequency range considered, with a drop in the sound reduction index at frequencies between 1000 and 2000 Hz. A laminated glass pane of the same thickness with an acoustic sheet can reduce this effect considerably (Fig. 3). The sound insulation of glazing also depends on the configuration of the panes and the bonds between them.

The acoustic effect of insulating glasses is based, on the one hand, on their higher weight per unit area – for this reason glasses > 6 mm thick are therefore mostly used – and, on the other, on the fact that a wider cavity increases the sound insulation, an aspect that can be further improved by filling the cavity with heavy gasses such as argon or krypton. As a rule, the sound insulation can be improved by about 3–5 dB, in some cases up to 8 dB. The best sound reduction indexes are achieved by including acoustic laminated glasses in such multi-pane insulating units (Fig. 4). However, the cavity contributes to the aforementioned drop in the sound insulation over certain frequency ranges because the gas infill transmits the vibrations from one pane to the other. One way of overcoming this is to use an asymmetrical pane configuration (different natural frequencies of the individual panes) (Fig. 5).

Furthermore, insulating glass is subjected to bowing and dishing effects, which are due to the different pressures in the cavity (fixed at the time of manufacture) and the surrounding air (constantly changing). The unavoidable fluctuations in the sound reduction index that can be expected lie in the range of 1–2 dB. Widening the cavity, using an asymmetrical pane configuration and employing thicker panes can all help to influence the sound reduction index R_w positively. It should be remembered here, however, that increasing the width of the cavity can reduce the thermal insulation effect. However, triple glazing is not necessarily a better sound insulator than double glazing (Fig. 6). The relationship between the sound insulating function and the width of the cavity and the thickness of the panes is not linear.

In summary, we can say that the level of sound insulation of multi-pane insulating glass is influenced in a diverse and complex manner by:
· Pane weight
· Pane stiffness
· Pane configuration
· Width of cavity
· Type of gas infill
Therefore, the effective sound reduction indexes cannot be determined by calculation, but instead only through tests. Such tests are carried out according to DIN EN 20140. However, adequate sound insulation is only achieved when it can be guaranteed that the frame to the glazing prevents sound transmissions through flanking components and impermeable joints prevent direct sound transmissions through the glazing component.

If, for example, a refurbishment project calls for the retention of windows with poor sound insulation properties, the DIN 4109 component method can be used to provide a rough estimate of the acoustic performance of the facade as a whole. In this approach, merely the ratio of the

areas of the individual components is considered. Large components with good sound insulation properties can help to compensate for smaller components with poorer sound insulation. DIN EN 12354 can be used to calculate the acoustic properties of buildings from the properties of the building components and also take into account the flanking transmissions. The results of the calculations according to DIN EN 12354 are therefore approximately equal to the sound insulation measured in situ according to DIN EN ISO 140-5.

Depending on the situation, acoustic glazing may need to satisfy additional requirements, e.g. act as a safety barrier. Owing to their low tear strength, acoustic sheets do not satisfy the requirements for laminated safety glass according to German Construction Products List A, part 1, annex 11.3. Proof of compliance with sound insulation and safety barrier requirements must therefore be assessed within the scope of an individual approval (ZiE), a national technical approval (abZ) or a national test certificate (abP) (see "Building legislation provisions", pp. 78–81).

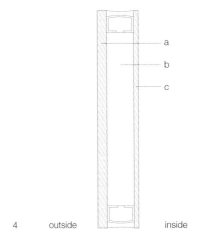

4   outside   inside

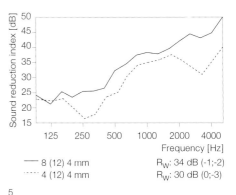

Sound reduction index [dB]

——— 8 (12) 4 mm R_W: 34 dB (-1;-2)
------ 4 (12) 4 mm R_W: 30 dB (0;-3)

5

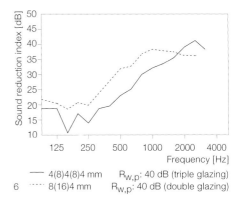

Sound reduction index [dB]

——— 4(8)4(8)4 mm $R_{W,P}$: 40 dB (triple glazing)
------ 8(16)4 mm $R_{W,P}$: 40 dB (double glazing)

6

1   Sound reduction index R_w of a window compared to the intensities of two noise sources: the window exhibits good sound insulation with respect to noise spectrum 1 but poor sound insulation with respect to noise spectrum 2.
2   Sound reduction indexes of single glazing
3   Sound reduction indexes of 8 mm thick glazing compared to laminated glass with a special acoustic sheet
4   Construction of sound insulating glazing: both widening the cavity between the panes and choosing an asymmetrical pane arrangement with a thicker outer pane can improve the sound reduction index.
    a Thick glass
    b Heavy gas filling
    c Thin glass
5   Sound reduction indexes of two acoustic glasses with symmetrical and asymmetrical cross-sections
6   Sound reduction indexes of two acoustic glasses with the same weighted sound reduction index

23

Safety, security

The most diverse impact-like loads caused by people or objects can subject glass to stresses and strains in various installation situations in many different ways. In principle, strengthened glasses such as heat-strengthened glass and toughened safety glass are much better than float glass at resisting impacts or damage to the surface. When we speak of safety glass we generally mean laminated safety glass (made from float glass or heat-strengthened glass) and toughened safety glass. Used overhead, for example, such types of glass have to guarantee that any objects falling onto the glass cannot break through. If the glass is destroyed, it must possess a residual loadbearing capacity for an adequate length of time and bind together the fragments so that any persons below are protected. Vertical glazing in public areas is generally also of safety glass in order to protect the people that assemble in such areas, possibly in great numbers. Glasses that also act as safety barriers (preventing persons falling from a higher to a lower level) must also pass the pendulum impact test in accordance with the Technical Rules for Glass in Safety Barriers (TRAV). This can be verified by tests, by selecting types of glass whose impact resistance has already been proved, or by calculation (see "Building legislation provisions", p. 81).

Security glazing includes anti-bandit, bullet-resistant and blast-resistant glasses. The use of polycarbonate sheets can be helpful when trying to reduce weight and avoid dangerous splinters (Fig. 1).

Anti-bandit glazing

Anti-bandit (also called anti-intruder, anti-vandal) security glasses can consist of a single, suitably thick pane, or several panes. The latter are laminated elements produced either entirely of glass or as a combination of glass and plastic. The majority of transparent or translucent glasses of this type, which if at all possible should not include any cutouts or openings, prevent the passage of thrown or impacting objects. They are intended to delay for a short time the effects of external violence on persons or objects in a protected zone. As long as the required resistance remains guaranteed, individual panes or interlayers can take on many different forms, e.g. with tints, coatings or printing. Furthermore, additional measures, e.g. improving the thermal insulation, determine the upgrading into a multi-pane insulating glass, and alarm or heating wires determine the total thickness and the visual appearance of the glazing. Such glazing must be fitted into frames that themselves provide suitable resistance to attack and can therefore support the glazing adequately and properly. DIN EN 356 specifies two methods for testing and classifying anti-bandit glazing.

Glazing resistant to manual attack (thrown objects) is divided into resistance classes P1A to P5A. Here, the classification depends on the height from which a hard body impactor (steel ball) weighing 4.11 kg is dropped onto horizontal glazing. In the test, the glazing must prevent the steel ball from penetrating. The greater the drop height, and hence the resulting energy the glass must resist, the higher the resistance class to which the glass is allocated.

In this simulation, the anti-bandit glass specimen is fixed in a standardised steel frame mounted on top of a container to catch the fragments and the steel ball. The test is carried out on three specimens, which must prevent the steel ball from penetrating.

Glazing resistant to manual attack (wielded objects) is assessed according to a simulated axe attack and allocated to classes

3

P6B to P8B accordingly. The simulation of the axe attack is carried out by means of a standardised mechanism. A distinction is made as to whether the attack is carried out with the blunt or sharp side of the axe. Three specimens must withstand a specified minimum number of impacts (which depends on the class) until the application of the external force creates a square opening measuring 400 × 400 mm (Fig. 2).

The classifications EN 356 P1A to EN 356 P8B designate anti-bandit glazing according to the standard and the level of resistance achieved. Fig. 1 shows two anti-bandit glasses of class P8B. A glass-only cross-section results in a 36 mm thick group of panes, whereas a glass/polycarbonate composite is just 24 mm thick and also results in a supporting construction that is up to 50 % lighter.

Bullet-resistant glazing
The main requirement to be satisfied by bullet-resistant glazing is the prevention of the penetration of projectiles from different types of weapons. Testing and classification is carried out according to DIN EN 1063 based on conventional weapons and types of ammunition. Bullet-resistant glazing can be made from glass and also plastic, but it must achieve a defined resistance to the penetration of projectiles. Bullet-resistant glazing can also form part of a multi-pane insulating glass unit. The standard specifies classes BR 1 to BR 7 for handguns and rifles plus SG 1 and SG 2 for shotguns. A distinction is made for the designated attack side depending on the distance of the weapon from the glass and the impact velocity for a specified number of hits. In addition, a 0.02 mm thick aluminium foil is set up parallel to the vertical test specimen and approx. 0.5 m behind it to serve as an indicator of any splinters that are ejected from the rear side of the test specimen.

Classification depends on whether the projectile or parts thereof damage the glazing or splinters of glass damage the foil. The glazing may not be penetrated. If the foil remains intact, the additional designation NS (no splinters) is added to the classification. If splinters are ejected and the foil is damaged, the letter S (splinters) is added. A bullet-resistant glazing product might therefore be designated, for example, EN 1063 BR 1 NS.

Blast-resistant glazing
The principal task of blast-resistant glazing is to protect people against the pressure waves of explosions. Like all other types of safety/security glazing products, the protective effect depends on the configuration of the glazing and its installation. The glass and/or plastic components of the glazing can also form part of a multi-pane insulating glass unit.

DIN EN 13541 describes the requirements and the general method of testing for the classification of blast-resistant glazing. Allocation to resistance classes ER 1 to ER 4 is carried out according to the maximum pressure forces generated and the duration of the pressure phase on the glazing. Glazing only passes the test when the pressure wave does not create any holes that pass right through the pane nor any openings between the fixing frame and the edge of the specimen. The methods for generating such a pressure wave are specified in DIN EN 13124 parts 1 and 2. Tests carried out on open ground or in a shock tube are possible (Fig. 3). In the case of open-air tests, the explosives are placed manually a few metres from the test specimen. As the pressure forces created by the explosion do not impact on the test surface uniformly, their uniformity is controlled approximately via the magnitude and arrangement of the explosive charge. In the shock tube tests, an

overpressure is generated in a chamber temporarily closed off by a membrane. After destruction of the membrane, the overpressure develops over the length of the shock tube into a vertical pressure wave that impacts on the vertical glazing with a uniform pressure. Shock tube tests are less time-consuming, are more cost-effective and easier to reproduce, but can only be used for assessing the behaviour of the glazing and its fixing in the frame. The test does not provide any information on the resistance of the surrounding components such as walls and floors, which is, however, possible within the scope of more extensive testing on open ground.

1   Class P8B anti-bandit glazing in the form of a pure glass laminate (36 mm thick) or as a glass/polycarbonate laminate (24 mm thick)
2   Testing anti-bandit glazing with a sharp axe
3   Shock tube test setup for testing blast-resistant glazing

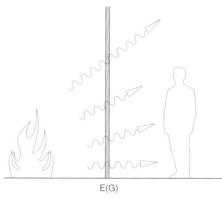

1

2

E(G)

Fire protection

General requirements

Fire protection represents an important aspect in the safety of the built environment. In Germany principal fire protection requirements are specified in the Model Building Code (MBO), which forms the basis for the building regulations of the individual federal states (LBO). In terms of fire protection, cl. 14 of the MBO calls for "buildings and structures to be planned, erected, modified and maintained in such a way that the outbreak of a fire and the spread of smoke and flames (propagation of fire) is prevented and in the event of a fire occurring it shall be possible to rescue people and animals and perform effective fire-fighting operations" (MBO, Nov 2002 edition).

The fire protection regulations of Germany's federal states differentiate between passive fire protection, which consists of constructional and organisational measures plus technical installations, and active measures in the form of fire-fighting.

The building materials and components used in buildings and structures must comply with certain requirements in order to achieve the goal of preventing the spread of fire. Building materials are divided into the following groups:
• incombustible
• not readily flammable
• flammable
Building components are divided into the following groups depending on their ability to withstand fire:
• fire-retardant
• highly fire-retardant
• fire-resistant
The assessment based on the building material leads to a statement regarding reaction to fire and the specification of a building materials class. The assessment based on the building component pro-vides information regarding the fire resistance and the fire resistance class. Allocation of these building authority designations to the designations used in the testing and classification standards of Germany's national standard DIN 4102 or Euronorm DIN EN 13501 is achieved via Construction Products List A part 1 and annexes 0.1ff. and 0.2ff.

The behaviour of glass in fire

Glass is generally incombustible and does not represent a fire load in the event of a fire. It is therefore allocated to building materials class A1 according to DIN 4102-4. The reaction to fire can be tested and evaluated according to DIN 4102-1. However, it is important to remember that when exposed to the effects of heat, normal sheet glass products shatter relatively easily because of their low tensile bending strength in conjunction with their relatively high coefficient of thermal expansion. Glass is therefore unsuitable for use in constructions designed to enclose an interior space and prevent the spread of fire. In order to obtain glass that provides effective fire protection, its breakage due to heat must either be ruled out or compensated for in some way.

Two types of glass – with different chemical compositions – are normally used for glass constructions: on the one hand, soda-lime-silica glass to DIN EN 572-1, on the other, borosilicate glass to DIN EN 1748-1-1. The chemical and physical properties of these glasses depend on their composition. Borosilicate glass is frequently used in fire protection applications because of its high ability to resist the stresses caused by temperature changes. This ability is based on the addition of 7–15 % boron oxide to the glass melt. The mean coefficient of thermal expansion α is $3.1–6.0 \times 10^{-6} \, K^{-1}$ instead of the $9.0 \times 10^{-6} \, K^{-1}$ of soda-lime-silica glass, which means that high temperature gradients lead to much lower stresses. Alkaline earth glasses according to DIN EN 14178-1 represent an alternative. Alkaline earths are mixed into the melt to produce these glasses, whose coefficient of thermal expansion ($8.0 \times 10^{-6} \, K^{-1}$) is slightly lower than that of soda-lime-silica glass. The use of glasses with a lower coefficient of thermal expansion can substantially reduce the stresses due to temperature changes.

So-called fire-resistant glasses are non-regulated building products in the meaning of Germany's building regulations. They either deviate considerably from the technical rules specified in Construction Products List A part 1, or there are no technical building regulations or generally acknowledged technical rules for these products. Their use therefore requires a

T2: Requirements to be satisfied by fire-resistant glazing to DIN 4102-13

F glazing	G glazing
Fire load according to standard temperature curve	
Glazing may not collapse due to its own weight	
Passage of smoke and fire must be prevented	
Glazing must remain as an effective enclosure • No flames on the side not directly exposed to the fire	
• Cotton wool pad held against element may not ignite or glow	
The temperature of the surface not directly exposed to the fire may not increase by more than 140 K (mean value) or 180 K (peak value).	

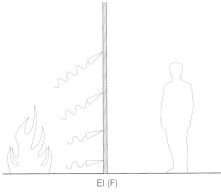

EI (F)

3

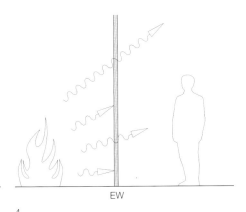

EW

4

national technical approval. However, a product approval cannot define any performance features that result from a particular installation. Building authorities therefore regulate the use of fire-resistant glass within the scope of an approval process for the type of fire-resistant glazing. The glazing closes openings in walls or serves for the construction of non-load-bearing walls and consists of frame, panes, glazing beads, seals and fasteners. Fire-resistant glazing must comply with specific requirements regarding stability, integrity and insulation. Compliance with these requirements must be verified by way of fire tests according to DIN 4102-13 or Euronorm DIN EN 1364.

The German edition of the Euronorm specifying the classification of building products and forms of construction with respect to the reaction to fire is DIN EN 13501. It is now possible to use the European classes for fire-resistant glazing within the scope of national approval procedures, provided positive fire test results according to the Euronorm are available. This means that glazing classes F and G have now been joined by classes EI and E respectively.

Despite the effects of fire, class G (E) glazing remains transparent and intact depending on the form of construction (Fig. 2). This class fulfils the sealing requirements even when installed as single glazing. In principle, this form of fire-resistant glazing prevents the passage of smoke and flames only. No requirements are specified regarding the transmission of heat and the ensuing radiant heat.

Class F (EI) glazing provides additional protection against the passage of heat radiation (Fig. 3) as well as preventing the spread of smoke and flames. The temperature on the side not directly exposed to

the fire may not increase by more than a certain amount. The improvement in the total thermal resistance is achieved by a multi-ply construction with special interlayers that foam up due to the effects of heat.

The construction of fire-resistant glazing
The frame may be of various materials, e.g. steel, wood, aluminium, reinforced concrete. The stability is guaranteed by continuous framing posts. Frame sections may be very narrow and may have different cross-sectional forms, although frameless constructions have also become available in the meantime – the panes of glass separated by silicone joints only.

The glazing beads for holding the fire-resistant glass in place must be made from incombustible materials, but, like the frames, various materials are possible. The glazing beads are generally fixed to the frames, and strips of sealing material to ensure non-rigid support for the panes of glass must be positioned between the glazing beads and the glass itself. These sealing strips may also provide a fire protection function by creating an insulating layer or foaming up in the event of a fire.

Glasses
The prefabricated panes of glass used for fire-resistant glazing are generally rectangular and flat, but other shapes and even bent glass may be used.

Class F (EI) glazing normally consists of at least two panes of float or toughened safety glass that are separated by a fire-resistant layer (Fig. 1). When exposed to heat, the pane on the fire side breaks. The gel, the fire-resistant layer, foams up and insulates the rest of the construction against the fire. Multi-ply glass blocks with a suitable web thickness and internal voids may also be used.

Class G (E) glazing employs special single glazing that, owing to its chemical composition and thermal toughening, is able to be used as part of a fire-resistant glazing unit providing sufficient resistance to the fire. This glazing does not shatter when exposed to fire, but instead deforms depending on the thermal load. Wired glass is frequently used. Furthermore, a glazing system can satisfy class G (E) requirements when it consists of at least two panes of float or toughened safety glass separated by a fire-resistant layer or by a cavity filled with air or a special gas. In the event of a fire, the fire-resistant layer also foams up. Glass blocks may also be used but the form of construction must be taken into account.

1 Construction of fire-resistant glazing
   a Glass
   b Gel
2 Fire-resistant glazing class E (G) prevents the passage of smoke and flames, but not the transmission of heat radiation.
3 Fire-resistant glazing class EI (F) prevents the passage of smoke, flames and heat radiation.
4 Fire-resistant glazing class EW prevents the passage of smoke and flames and reduces the transmission of heat radiation.

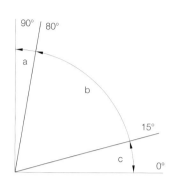

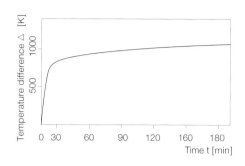

Installation positions and variations
DIN 4102-13 makes a distinction between vertical, sloping or horizontal installations depending on the angle between the glass and a horizontal plane (Fig. 2). Wall openings and walls corresponding to the vertical installation position must guarantee the fire protection requirements for a fire on either side. For sloping or horizontal fire-resistant glazing in suspended floors and roofs, the fire protection requirements must be satisfied for a fire from below.

Fire-resistant glazing can be used in single openings, as a continuous row of windows or as a partition. In the case of a single opening, a pane of glass is fixed in a peripheral frame. With continuous rows of windows or partitions, several panes of glass are positioned adjacent to each other vertically and/or horizontally.

Fire protection tests
Building products and forms of construction are classified with the help of DIN EN 13501 by means of fire tests. The fire resistance tests for loadbearing and non-loadbearing components are regulated by DIN EN 1363 to 1365. The tests are always carried out on the complete fire-resistant glazing element, generally full size, and according to the installation situation. After the fire-resistant glazing has been installed in the test setup in the furnace, the test is carried out according to a prescribed procedure involving a standard temperature curve (Fig. 3). The assessment of the duration of fire resistance is carried out according to the most unfavourable result achieved in two fire tests on specimens of the fire-resistant glazing involved.

Class E glazing is smoke-tight and flameproof, i.e. provides an effective barrier to the passage of smoke and flames. Any gaps or openings that ensue may not exceed a certain size. In addition, and in contrast to class G glazing, a pad of cotton wool held against the side not directly exposed to the fire may not ignite spontaneously.

In the case of EI glazing, which in addition must insulate against the heat of a fire, the temperature of the surface of the glass on the side not directly exposed to the fire may not rise above the room temperature at the start of the test by more than 140 K on average and at no time more than 180 K as a peak value. As soon as the loadbearing or enclosing functions are no longer satisfied, the thermal insulation criterion is also no longer relevant, irrespective of whether the above temperature limits have been complied with.

Coated fire-resistant glazing (EW glazing) reduces, in particular, the passage of heat radiation (p. 27, Fig. 4). To comply with this requirement, the radiation generated by a fire may not exceed 15 kW/m² when measured at a distance of 1 m from the surface not directly exposed to the fire. If a fire-resistant glazing element fails due to the emergence of gaps and openings, fire can spread to the side not directly exposed to the fire. The enclosing func-

T3: Requirements to be satisfied by fire-resistant glazing to DIN EN 357

Criterion, code letter	Definition for describing the fire resistance ability
Stability R	… is the ability of a component to withstand a fire load from one or more sides for a certain length of time without becoming unstable.
Integrity E	… is the ability of a component with an enclosing function to withstand a fire load from one side only. Propagation of the fire to the side not directly exposed as a result of the passage of flames or a considerable quantity of hot gases, which could lead to ignition of the side not directly exposed or neighbouring materials, is prevented.
Radiant heat reduction W	… is the ability of a component with an enclosing function to withstand a fire load from one side only such that the heat radiation measured on the side not directly exposed to the fire remains below a specified value for a certain length of time.
Insulation I	… is the ability of an element to withstand a fire load from one side only without propagation of the fire as a result of considerable heat conduction from the fire side to the other side, which could lead to ignition of the side not directly exposed or neighbouring materials. This also means that the element provides an adequate heat barrier for protecting people in the vicinity of the element for the period of time associated with the classification.
Smoke stop S	… is the ability of an element to limit the passage of hot or cold gases or smoke from one side to the other.
Self-closing C	… is the ability of a closure to close off an opening by some device either after every opening action or upon the occurrence of fire or smoke.

1 Glazing during a fire test
2 Installation positions of fire-resistant glazing to DIN 4102-13
   a Vertical glazing, 80° to 90°
   b Sloping glazing, > 15° to 80°
   c Horizontal glazing, 0° to 15°
3 Standard temperature curve – the basis of all fire tests
4 Energy and daylight balance for a 4 mm thick glass pane with respect to the range of visible wavelengths

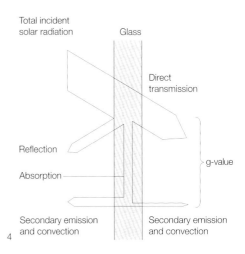

4

tion and hence the reduction in the transmission of heat radiation is then no longer satisfied.

The results recorded during a fire test must always be evaluated taking into account the adjoining components.

Thermal insulation and solar control

Buildings or rooms intended for occupation by people must be adequately insulated against heat losses in the winter and overheating in the summer in order to create comfortable and hygienic living conditions. Thermal insulation and solar-control measures reduce the energy consumption requirements for heating in winter and cooling in summer. In the case of thermal insulation, we distinguish between the summertime and wintertime thermal performance. The primary task of wintertime thermal performance is to limit the transmission heat losses through the building components. DIN EN 673 uses thermal transmittance values (U-values) to express this performance. A U-value specifies the magnitude of the heat flow through 1 m^2 of a planar building component for an air temperature difference of 1 K between the two sides of that component (normally inside and outside). DIN 4108 lays down the limit values for thermal transmittance. Solar gains through areas of glass have a positive influence on the energy requirements during the heating period, but during the summer they contribute substantially to unwanted heating of the interior. In order to guarantee a pleasant interior climate, we must either limit the amount of incoming solar radiation or install building services, which, however, could lead to an undesirable increase in the energy consumption.

The energy permeability of a glazing element is specified by the total energy transmittance (g-value), which describes the ratio of the incident radiation to that

which reaches the interior by way of transmission and secondary heat emissions (Fig. 4). Besides solar radiation, the room temperature is also dependent on the following factors:
- Size of room
- Orientation and size of windows
- Type of glazing
- Type of sunshading
- Ventilation behaviour of users
- Internal heat sources
- Heat capacity of components, especially internal components

The multi-pane insulating glass to DIN EN 1279 normally used in the building envelope today can have a wide range of functional and optical properties. The construction of this derived glass product plus the possible coatings are described in "Basic glass and derived products" (pp. 15 and 18–19).

Physical principles
We divide the total solar radiation into three spectral ranges relevant for the building industry: ultraviolet radiation with wavelengths from 280 to 380 nm, visible light (380–780 nm) and the heat radiation of the near infrared range (780–2800 nm). The main properties of multi-pane insulating glasses are described by the radiation variables reflectance ρ, transmittance τ and absorptance α. Depending on the angle of incidence and the position of the coating in the multi-pane make-up, part of the incoming radiation is reflected at the boundary surface between the gaseous and the solid medium and part is transmitted through the glass; another part is absorbed by the glass. The absorption, reflection and transmission components together add up to 100 %. We use the light transmittance τ_v to assess the daylight factor, which in the form of a percentage describes how much of the visible radiation passes through the

glazing. All these physical variables can be influenced by tinting or coating the glass. They are determined as mean values by measurements or according to DIN EN 410. Float glass is impermeable to radiation below 300 nm and above 2500 nm, and absorbs such wavelengths. Another important variable for glass is the emissivity ε, which is the ability of a body to emit energy in the form of radiation. It is calculated according to DIN EN 673. Although glass is impermeable to longwave radiation, the absorbed energy can be very easily re-emitted in the form of heat. Glass therefore possesses a high emissivity.

Multi-pane insulating and low E glass
Thermal insulation is essentially based on the thermal resistances of the materials used and the resistances of their surfaces. Glass is, in principle, a good conductor of heat. Multi-layer glass elements therefore represent an attempt to minimise the heat losses during the heating period by introducing buffering cavities between the panes. Such products are designated multi-pane insulating glasses, but we generally refer to them as double glazing, triple glazing, etc. Multi-pane insulating glasses with cavities filled with a noble gas achieve U-values between 1.0 and about 2.2 W/m^2K. In the case of triple glazing (two cavities) plus a noble gas, U-values between 0.5 and 0.8 W/m^2K are possible.

About two-thirds of the heat losses are due to heat radiation from the warm to the cold side. The remaining third is made up of convection losses plus conduction losses via the filling in the cavity and the edge seal to the insulating unit, which acts as a thermal bridge (p. 30, Fig. 1). Improving the thermal insulation effect of multi-pane insulating glass is therefore based on reducing the large

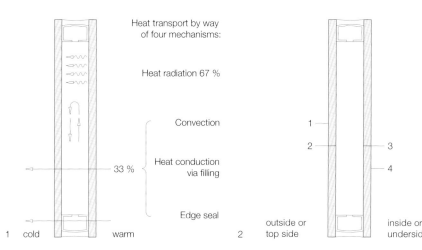

Heat transport by way
of four mechanisms:

Heat radiation 67 %

Convection

Heat conduction
via filling

Edge seal

33 %

1   cold   warm   2   outside or
top side   inside or
underside

1 ─
2 ─   ─ 3
─ 4

heat losses due to radiation. To this end, thin (0.01–1.0 mm) layers of noble metals (copper, silver, gold) are applied to the surfaces in the cavity in the online method, or semiconductor materials (tin oxide) are sprayed on (Fig. 3). These so-called low E (= emissivity) coatings improve the radiation properties of the glass by reducing the emissivity of the coated glass surface. Low E glazing is therefore a glazing unit with a low E coating applied to at least one pane. As, above all, the coatings applied in the offline process – independent of the float glass process – exhibit a poor resistance to atmospheric and mechanical effects, they must always be positioned in the cavity. The thermal insulation properties of the glazing (U-value) depend on the configuration of the insulating glass (double, triple), the gas filling in the cavity, the nature and number of coatings and the emissivity of the glazing. Whether coated or uncoated multi-pane insulating glass is used essentially depends on the type of building and the building physics concept. In Germany the strict energy conservation stipulations mean that noble gas fillings (e.g. argon) and coated multi-pane insulating glasses are mostly encountered these days. It should be remembered that the thermal insulation effect of a window must always be considered in conjunction with its frame. Abrasion-resistant online coatings – i.e. those applied in conjunction with the float glass process – are possible on single glazing but are generally used only for refurbishing single-glazed windows or for replacing secondary glazing.

In order to achieve additional solar energy gains during the heating period, the glazing must permit the passage of ample solar energy (high g-value) and daylight (high τ_v value). As coatings absorb some of the solar radiation, reducing the U-value at the same time lowers the total energy and light transmittance values. A compromise between thermal insulation and passive energy gains is achieved with a g-value of 65 % and a simultaneous daylight factor τ_v of about 60 %. Better thermal insulation with its simultaneous maximum solar gains (g = 65 %) can be achieved by applying an infrared-reflective coating to the inner pane (Fig. 2, layer 3). The coating specifically prevents heat emissions from the inner to the outer pane of the insulating unit – and the retained heat is absorbed and re-emitted into the interior. However, applying a similar coating to the inside of the outer pane (Fig. 2, layer 2) results in a g-value of only about 56 %. The effectiveness of the coating therefore depends on its position in the multi-pane insulating unit, which is why the panes of insulating glass must be marked accordingly in the factory.

Solar-control glass
As the U-value of a glazing unit can be reduced very considerably, large areas of thermally insulating glass are now possible in architecture. However, in summer this can lead to overheating of the interior due to excessive solar gains. The aim of the summertime thermal performance is therefore to minimise the total energy transmittance (g-value), which, however, is contrary to the aim of wintertime thermal performance! Finding the best compromise for a particular building is therefore essential. But minimising the incoming energy through solar-control measures has a negative effect on the daylight factor. Typical solar-control glasses – either tinted products or those with a reflective coating – have a g-value of about 50 % and a light transmittance of approx. 40 %. Tinted glasses absorb a large proportion of the incoming radiation, which, after a delay, is then re-emitted to the surroundings in the form of heat. The effect depends on the degree of tinting and the thickness of the glass. This approach allows the g-value to be decreased to 30 %. As absorptive glasses experience a quite severe rise in temperature, only toughened glasses should be used. Solar-control glasses with a reflective coating function by reflecting a large part of the incoming solar radiation back from the coated surface so that it does not enter the interior. Such glasses undergo only a minor increase in temperature. The reflective coatings can be applied using both online and offline methods. Online coatings achieve an excellent solar-control effect, but cannot improve the thermal insulation behaviour of the glazing at the same time. Such coatings are used for the outer panes of multi-pane insulating glasses and can be combined with a thermally insulating inner pane. So-called sunbelt layers with double functions can be produced using the offline process (Fig. 4). These are characterised by their solar-control and thermal insulation prop-

T4: Relationship between thermal transmittance (U-value) and glass configuration (examples)

Configuration of glass	Thermal transmittance U-value [W/m²K]
6 mm float glass, uncoated	5.7
2 No. 6 mm float glass, uncoated, 12 mm cavity	2.8
2 No. 6 mm float glass, uncoated, 15 mm cavity (air)	1.4
2 No. 6 mm float glass, uncoated, 15 mm cavity (argon)	1.2

3

4

erties. The thermal insulation is achieved by an intermediate layer of silver, which reduces the emissivity of the glass. The reflective property, i.e. the solar-control effect, is regulated by way of metal oxides applied over the whole area of the glass. However, such coatings are less hardwearing and are therefore applied mostly to the inside surface of the outer pane (Fig. 2, layer 2) of an insulating glass unit. A solar-control effect can also be achieved by applying silk-screen printing to the glass: the surface of the glass is partly shaded by printing, which results in reduced radiation transmission. The effectiveness depends on the ratio of transparent to non-transparent surfaces and the degree of absorption. However, the daylight factor is also reduced to the same extent.

Additional sunshading
To achieve protection from excessive sunlight, glazing can be used in conjunction with other measures. We distinguish here between internal, external and cavity sunshading systems. Sunshades fitted outside can effectively block the incident radiation energy even before it reaches the glazing. Such systems include permanent or movable blinds of metal, wood, plastics or glass. If an external mechanical shade is highly reflective and at the same time lightweight, the cooling requirement in summer can be cut by up to 60 %. However, as such systems are usually impermeable to light, it becomes necessary to use artificial lighting in the building, which in turn has a negative effect on the energy balance. Another approach is to fit additional elements such as roller blinds, louvre blinds, stretched fabrics or even photovoltaic elements in the cavity between the inner and outer panes. Such arrangements require a sufficiently wide cavity and vertical or near-vertical glazing, otherwise contact with the glass can

impair the functioning of such sunshades. Integral photovoltaic elements are mostly applied to a backing material using casting resin. They function as sunshades, but at the same time generate electricity! Stretched materials in the cavity help to increase the sunshading effect and decrease the U-value by dividing the cavity into two parts. Furthermore, special inlays (spun glass, non-woven fabrics, perforated sheet metals) between the inner and outer panes have a positive influence on the solar-control and thermal insulating effects of the glazing. Sunshades fitted inside, e.g. curtains, or plastic sheets glued to the glass, can only reflect the solar radiation. Absorbed radiation components remain in the room as heat. Such measures are therefore more suitable as anti-glare screens. The absorbed radiation, especially if the system is fitted too close to the glass, can lead to a severe thermal load on the pane. Large restraint stresses can build up due to the different temperatures between the middle of the pane and at the partially shaded edges of the glass. In some circumstances it is therefore necessary to use thermally toughened glass. Internal sunshading alone can reduce the cooling requirements by max. 30 %.

1   Heat transport in an insulating glass unit
2   The sequence of layers used in practice for insulating glass units; the position of the coating is designated by the numbers 1–4 from outside to inside.
3   Coating bonded directly to the glass surface using the online method
4   Offline coating for thermal insulation and solar control
    a Protective layer (e.g. SnO_2, ZnO)
    b Effective layer (e.g. NiCr, TiO_2)
    c Effective layer (e.g. Ag)
    d Bonding to glass (e.g. SnO_2, ZnO)

Designing with glass

Glass performs numerous different tasks in building applications. The most important of these are allowing daylight into the interior of a building, enabling views into and out of a building and at the same time providing protection against the weather. However, today's architecture places additional demands on this popular building material; above all, the growing desire for "dematerialised" building components calls for innovative constructional solutions because as glass replaces more and more opaque building materials, it has to fulfil more and more diverse requirements (p. 34, Fig. 4). The sizes of building components are increasing and new applications appearing. This means that aspects that in traditional applications, e.g. windows, played only a minor role now have to be given more and more attention.

Large areas of glass are frequently the outcome of demanding architectural concepts. However, whether one component or a whole building is perceived as transparent depends on many different factors.

The relationships affecting the use of glass in buildings are therefore explained in this chapter.

Optics and perception

The term "optics" designates the study of light. Light is generally understood as being that visible to the human eye. This so-called visible spectrum is a relatively narrow portion of the electromagnetic spectrum covering the wavelengths from about 380 to 780 nm, the so-called visible spectrum. When light strikes a body, radiation components are reflected, absorbed and transmitted depending on the properties of the material and its surfaces, the respective wavelength and the angle of incidence. According to the law of conservation of energy, the sum of these three components is equal to the total amount of incident light (see "Glass for special requirements", p. 29, Fig. 4). In the case of a typical pane of soda-lime-silica float glass 4 mm thick and an angle of incidence of 90°, approx. 8 % (4 % per surface) is reflected, 90 % transmitted and 2 % absorbed.

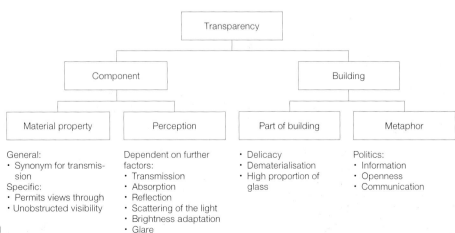

1   Different meanings of the term "transparency"   1

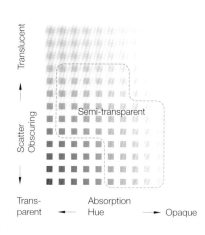

1

2

3

Transmission, opacity

Transmission describes the permeability of a material by electromagnetic radiation. Light-permeable materials generally exhibit varying degrees of transmission for various wavelengths. Within the range of visible light, the human eye perceives this variation as a coloured hue. Float glass with an average iron oxide content of 0.1%, for example, absorbs light primarily in the range of red light – the glass therefore takes on a greenish colouring, which is particularly evident at the edges. But the degree of transmission (transmittance) is only a measure of the quantitative passage of radiation, not the quality of the light transmitted. So the way the light is scattered, for example, is ignored. Opacity is another term used to describe the light permeability of a material. An opaque material is impermeable to light.

Reflection and refraction

Some optical effects occur directly at the surface of light-permeable materials. When light strikes a boundary surface between two media with different optical densities and low absorption properties (e.g. air and glass), it is split into two components:

one part is reflected, whereas the other part enters the other medium at an angle different to the angle of incidence. This change of direction is known as refraction. When the light exits an element with parallel surfaces, the refractive alteration is reversed, i.e. the original angle is restored, so that, in total, the light has undergone only a minor parallel translation. This is usually only evident in a direct comparison with an unglazed surface, such as when a window is open.

According to the law of reflection, the angle of incidence is equal to the angle of reflection. If the surface is smooth in comparison to the wavelengths of visible light, then this reflection is perceived as regular – the reflected image appears bright and in focus (Fig. 5a). A diffuse, dull reflection occurs when the reflecting surface is uneven – the rays of light are reflected in different directions, i.e. scattered (Fig. 5b), which results in a blurred image. When light re-emerges from a pane of glass, total reflection occurs above a certain angle. For glass, this angle is about 42° (measured from a line perpendicular to the surface of the glass). [1]

Transparency, translucency, semi-transparency

Glass is generally thought of as a transparent material; however, depending on the specialist discipline, the term "transparency" can take on different meanings. In physics, for example, transparency is a synonym for transmission: transparency specifies the wavelengths for which a material is permeable, and to which extent. But once again, this says nothing about the quality of the radiation transmission, i.e. whether the light is transmitted in diffuse, scattered form or directly. Transparency in terms of physics is therefore a property of a material or building component which is not dependent on external factors. In contrast to this, transparency in architecture refers not only to the light permeability of a material or building component, but also to the ability to perceive images through that material or building component. This is the case, when, in addition to a high non-diffuse radiation transmission, the degree of reflection (reflectance) is relatively low.

With a high degree of absorption (absorptance) but otherwise a non-diffuse radia-

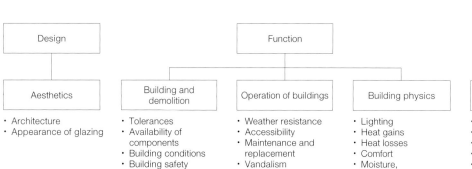

Design		Function		Loadbearing structure	
Aesthetics	Building and demolition	Operation of buildings	Building physics	Loadbearing capacity and serviceability	Safety requirements
· Architecture · Appearance of glazing	· Tolerances · Availability of components · Building conditions · Building safety · Erection sequence · Demolition · Replacement	· Weather resistance · Accessibility · Maintenance and replacement · Vandalism · Durability · Usage · Economy	· Lighting · Heat gains · Heat losses · Comfort · Moisture, condensation · Sound insulation · Sustainability	· Static loads · Impact loads · Deformations · Failure behaviour · Restraints	· Anti-intruder measures · Bullet resistance · Blast resistance · Fire protection

4

tion transmission, we speak of a hue or tinge of colour. Materials that transmit light but also scatter it, either at their surfaces or within their cross-section, are no longer transparent, but hazy or (partly) obscured, i.e. translucent. The use of the term semi-transparent is ambiguous. It can be applied to non-transparent or lightly coloured materials that appear transparent or translucent to a certain extent. The transitions between transparency, translucency and toning or haziness are in no way constant (Fig. 3).

Light and the sense of vision
Various physical, physiological and psychological effects lead to an object that is transparent in the architectural sense not always being perceived as such in the literal sense of the word, even though the transparency, as a material property, has not changed. When observed in daylight from a certain distance, the closed windows of a fenestrate facade often appear dark grey. This happens, even though the building is occupied and the persons inside the building are of the opinion they are in bright surroundings and can enjoy an undisturbed view out through the windows. Bright objects or surfaces near the windows remain discernible from outside (Fig. 8), but not objects further back from the windows. The way human beings perceive their surroundings visually is therefore also important in addition to the purely physical properties of building components.

Of the many variables and units used in lighting engineering, luminance – the basis for our perception of brightness besides the spectral composition of the light as the starting point for the effect of colour – represents one of the most important factors affecting our visual perception of our surroundings. Luminance is defined as the luminous intensity per unit area. The

human eye is able to adjust to extreme differences in luminance amounting to more than six powers of 10. This process is known as brightness adaptation.

Perception of contrast
Although our sense of vision allows us to see over a wide range of absolute luminance levels, our brains can process only a comparatively narrow range of relative luminance levels within a certain setting. In bright surroundings, an area of medium luminance will appear brighter than in darker surroundings (Fig. 6). Our perception of brightness is therefore closely related to the brightness adaptation of the eye. Furthermore, the contrast between two neighbouring surfaces with different luminance levels is augmented at the boundary between those surfaces (Fig. 7). [2]

a Regular (or specular) reflection   b Diffuse reflection

5

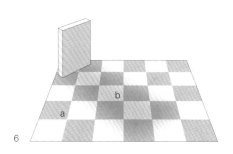

6

7

1, 2   Different perceptions of transparency depending on the luminance available; Burda Media Tower, Offenburg (D), 1998, Ingenhoven, Overdiek & Partner
3   Definitions of terminology: transparency, translucency and opacity in conjunction with their transitional phenomena
4   Design and planning criteria for glass in building
5   Schematic presentation of types reflection depending on the surface properties
6   Relativity of the perception of brightness depending on the surroundings; in reality fields a and b have the same grey-scale value.
7   Perception of contrast gain by means of the so-called Mach bands: although every field is a uniform shade, each appears lighter along its left border.
8   Playing with the visual effect of glass: in reality the constructional grid does not consist of rhombuses, but rather triangles and trapeziums. However, the white-painted diagonals behind the outer leaf are more prominent visually. Office building, 30 St Mary Axe, London (GB), 2004, Foster + Partners

8

Glare

Besides brightness and contrast, various types of glare play a major role when using glass in buildings. Disabling glare occurs when luminance levels within the field of vision are so great that they exceed the maximum adaptation ability of the eye and protective reflexes take effect, e.g. like when we look directly at the sun. Discomforting glare occurs when there is a sudden, substantial change in the luminance level within the field of vision following a prior, longer period of adaptation of the eye to a different luminance level. That is the case when we move from a dark room into bright daylight. Direct glare is caused by the relatively high luminance level of a confined area within the field of vision, e.g. a bright lamp or sunlight shining on a surface. Reflected glare is triggered by reflections from light sources. The degree of glare also depends on the information content of the surface observed. Even in the case of a high luminance contrast between a window and the adjacent walls, an interesting view is perceived as less affected by glare than the luminance of a correspondingly diffuse and translucent surface. [3]

Transparency of building sections

Just as the perception of the transparency of a building component is heavily dependent on the lighting conditions of its surroundings, the degree of transparency of a whole part of a building – especially its facade – cannot be evaluated without considering its construction. As already explained, the brightness adaptation and "contrast gain" of the human eye and brain can lead to the otherwise slightly greenish edges of glass elements appearing as dark lines against a bright background (Fig. 1).

The degree of transparency of a facade can be expressed as the quotient of the truly transparent and highly absorbent or opaque areas. But, irrespective of this ratio, the number, arrangement and size of non-transparent facade elements can influence the impression of transparency. A highly resolved, intricate construction can appear considerably less transparent than a comparable building with fewer facade elements with larger cross-sections (Fig. 2). On the other hand, a small-format loadbearing construction can divide a facade and provide it with depth and expression. [4]

Measures to reinforce the impression of transparency

Changing the physical-optical material properties can increase the transparency of a glazed construction at the level of the building component. This can be achieved by reducing the absolute reflectance with the help of suitable anti-reflection treatments or by reducing the absorptance through the use of low-iron, extra-clear glass. On the architectural level, precisely planned lighting or the provision of bright surfaces behind a facade can increase the impression of transparency. In order to prevent disturbing reflections, the entire facade can be angled towards a dark soffit or a dark floor. This principle is often employed for the facades of car showrooms or airport control towers. Severe luminance contrasts within the field of vision should be avoided.

Transparency as a metaphor

The term transparency is frequently used in a figurative sense to describe the openness of governmental or political institutions; an aspect they then try to convey through the architecture of their buildings. The forms of construction chosen are intended to allow passers-by and visitors generous insights into those buildings and the internal workflows (Fig. 6).

1 An all-glass facade with a high degree of transparency: the glazing appears as a delicate, dematerialised skin; Sainsbury Centre for Visual Arts, Norwich (GB), 1978, Foster Associates
2 Facades extremely resolved in constructional terms can suffer from impaired transparency at certain viewing angles and under certain lighting conditions; Stadttor, Dusseldorf (D), 1998, Overdiek, Petzinka & Partner (competition, draft design, building permission application), Petzinka Pink & Partner (final design, realisation)
3 Severe luminance contrast between external wall and interior plus reflected glare make glazing appear grey and opaque during daylight.
4 At night the glazing is opaque in the opposite direction.
5 Schematic presentation of the glare at a pane of glass during daylight: the reflections on the outside of the glazing (Rh) suppress visual information from the interior (Td); multi-pane insulating glass reinforces this effect.
6 The metaphor in construction: the use of transparent building components in parliamentary and governmental buildings is intended to symbolise openness and accessibility for the citizens; interior view of the plenary chamber at the Saxony parliament building in Dresden (D),1997, Peter Kulka

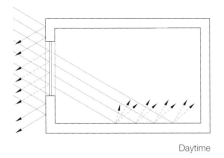

Daytime

3

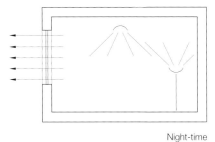

Night-time

4

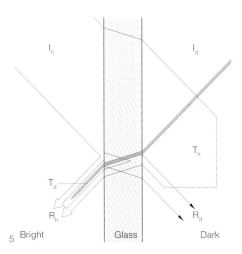

5 Bright   Glass   Dark

Optical impairments of glass products

A number of the optical properties of glass products can be specifically controlled for their applications in building. These include tinting or the removal of all colour via the chemical composition of the glass melt, or subsequent surface treatments such as sand-blasting or etching. In addition, optical phenomena can occur that are particularly conspicuous in the use of glass in building because even minimal geometrical deviations from a perfectly flat facade surface can distort reflected images and views through the glass. Although such flaws are frequently undesirable, the physical properties of the material make this unavoidable in principal. They are thus not "defects" in the sense of construction law.

Bowing and dishing effects
One optical phenomenon is frequently observed in conjunction with the use of insulating glass units. As the individual panes of such units are hermetically sealed, pressure differences between the surrounding air and the gas or air in the cavity between the panes leads to volume changes. This results in convex or concave deformations of the panes of glass (p. 38, Figs. 1 and 2). The extent of this change in volume is determined by:
- Atmospheric pressure fluctuations due to meteorological conditions
- Temperature fluctuations
- Pressure and temperature differences between place of manufacture and place of installation

Besides the visible phenomena, climatic changes place loads on the individual panes. The following applies in principle: the larger the format and the thinner the pane, the lower the resulting loads due to climatic changes – but the greater the effects on the optical quality.

Anisotropy and double refraction
Homogeneous, evenly cooled sheet glass is isotropic in the optical sense, i.e. it exhibits the same optical properties in all directions. However, even when closely spaced, the jets of air used in the thermal toughening process cool the surface of the glass unevenly, leading to glass with anisotropic optical qualities. Polarised light, incident on the surface at an angle other than 90°, is split into two waves.

6

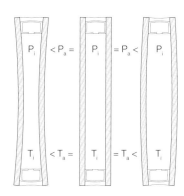

$P_i < P_a = $ $P_i = P_a < $ P_i

$T_i < T_a = $ $T_i = T_a < $ T_i

1

2

This effect is known as double refraction (or birefringence). Under certain lighting conditions this phenomenon usually manifests itself as a stripy pattern corresponding to the arrangement of the air jets (Fig. 3).

Interference phenomena
Interference is the superposition of two or more waves at one point. Interference phenomena are rare in glass applications in building and only occur with several parallel panes of float glass, one behind the other (e.g. insulating glass), under certain lighting conditions. The interference manifests itself as stripy zones split into the colours of the spectrum, the positions of which change as the individual panes deform. As the occurrence of interference requires that the surfaces of the panes be perfectly parallel, this phenomenon must be regarded as an indication of excellent float glass quality!

Coatings
Surface coatings for controlling the building physics properties of glass, e.g. low E coatings, can lead to coloured reflections depending on the lighting conditions and the position of the observer. Generally, however, they allow a view through the glass without distorting the colours (see "Glasses for special requirements", pp. 29–31).

Roller indentations ("roller waves")
A wavy surface is a phenomenon that is particularly prevalent with thermally toughened glasses. The hot glass rests on rollers during the toughening process, which can lead to deviations from an ideally flat surface. The waves manifest themselves in a distortion of the reflected image.

Lens effect
If panes of glass with roller waves are further processed to form laminated safety glass,

an unlucky superposition of the unevenness can cause an optical lens effect, which leads to a convex or concave distortion of the view through the glass.

Structural concepts
The use of glass as a construction material differs fundamentally from the use of many other building materials. Owing to the brittle failure behaviour of glass, exceeding its loadbearing capacity results in the sudden and complete failure of the component (see "Basic glass and derived products", p. 11, Fig. 1). In addition, it reacts very sensitively to local stress peaks and has a very low impact strength. Once a crack has started to form, it can propagate unhindered owing to the molecular structure of glass. Another negative characteristic of glass, in addition to its problematic brittle failure behaviour, is the fact that upon failure it shatters into a multitude of sharp pieces that represent a further potential danger. These properties result in far-reaching consequences for the use of glass in building. Building materials such as steel or reinforced concrete are much less problematic because they exhibit a ductile behaviour at the temperatures relevant to construction, meaning that local stress peaks can be dissipated via plastic deformations. Such deformations therefore usually provide advance warning of the imminent failure of a ductile building component.

Safety and risks
Safety concepts for buildings are typically based on building legislation stipulations or particular safety objectives determined by clients and users. Those include valuable operational facilities, irreplaceable museum exhibits, or the building itself. Generally, however, the protection of persons is assigned maximum priority. Expressed in simple terms, the risk aris-

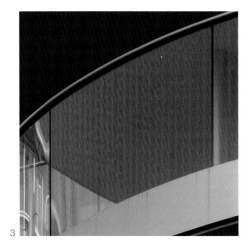

3

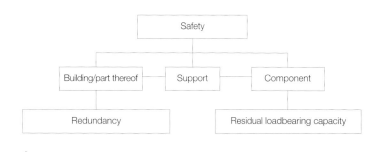

4

ing from a building construction can be considered to be the product of the probability of the occurrence of component failure and its effect on the building as a whole. In order to minimise the risk of failure of the loadbearing structure, it is possible to increase the functional safety of a building component and also limit the consequences of its failure. In most cases, the absolute safety for a glass building component (safe-life concept) is not possible for economic, architectural and technical reasons. However, it must always be guaranteed that, should a component fail, sufficient time remains to bring the persons and property to be protected to safety and not endanger those carrying out rescue operations (fail-safe concept). The failure of a single component should never trigger a chain reaction that leads to the collapse of the entire construction. Any defects in components must be detectable during regular, routine inspections and maintenance work.

Residual loadbearing capacity
Appropriate measures must be taken to prevent the sudden collapse of an entire construction and total failure of a glass component. Even in the case of damage, a glass component must possess sufficient loadbearing reserves in order to remain securely in position and still withstand other loads, e.g. falling persons or objects, for a sufficient length of time. Furthermore, the splinters and fragments of glass must be bonded together in such a way that there is no danger of pieces of broken glass falling onto persons below, nor a serious risk of injury to persons who may fall onto the broken pane of glass. The margin of safety against complete failure of a partially destroyed system is known as the residual loadbearing capacity. This is one of the most important aims when using glass in construction (Fig. 4) and, in principle, can only be achieved

with the help of other, ductile materials. These materials, such as the polyvinyl butyral (PVB) film that holds together the pieces of broken glass, can be virtually invisible.

Redundancy
In principle, glass structures should be designed with inherent redundancies, i.e. upon failure of one loadbearing element in a system, the loads can be carried by other elements in the loadbearing construction. Failure scenarios for the glazing must be investigated within the scope of the structural analysis in order to verify the safety of the system. Besides the residual loadbearing capacity, redundancy represents the most important safety principle in the use of glass as a structural material.

Hierarchical systems
Glass components can be incorporated in a loadbearing structure in many ways. We distinguish between primary and secondary structural elements, and infilling, tertiary glass elements, depending on whether or not the glass element is assigned a loadbearing function within the system. Allocating the building components to different groups according to their task within the overall construction is based on a structural concept known as a hierarchical system. Such a system is characterised by the fact that the components of the different hierarchy levels fulfil different tasks and are therefore inferior or superior to other levels. These tasks are divided into load-carrying and load-applying functions. In a hierarchical system, forces are grouped together so that the loads increase from top to bottom, while the number of elements decreases. In terms of calculations, hierarchical systems are comparatively easy to handle, and the flow of forces is frequently readily discernible (p. 40, Fig. 2).

The structural carcass normally constitutes the primary structure, the main loadbearing system of a building. Even partial failure of the primary structure will result in serious consequences for the structural behaviour of the construction as a whole, or at least a large part of it. The stability of a primary loadbearing element for a certain length of time is therefore essential in the case of a major disaster. Glass elements cannot usually comply with such functional safety requirements – or if they must, then only with the help of elaborate, costly arrangements and additional safety measures, which in the end call into question the very use of the glass as a transparent, dematerialising building material. It is for this reason that glass has been used for the primary structure of only a handful of buildings to date – and none more than one storey high.

The secondary structure is made up of elements that carry loads from tertiary items and, in turn, transfer these plus their own loads to the primary structure. It therefore serves as an intermediate level between primary and tertiary structures. A supporting framework for a facade represents a typical secondary structure. Finally, the tertiary structure comprises all

1 Sketch of the principle of the bowing and dishing of an insulating glass unit: pressure differences between the outside air and the gas in the cavity result in deformations of the panes which can lead to distorted reflections.
2 Panes distorted by pressure differences manifest themselves as distorted reflections in a glass facade
3 The double refraction effect manifests itself as a stripy pattern on a glass balustrade
4 Elementary safety concepts in the use of glass as a structural element: redundancy and residual loadbearing capacity

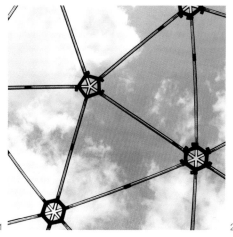

1

2

the components in the outer building envelope and normally consists of infilling, enclosing elements that carry only their own weight plus weather-induced loads and transfer these to the secondary structure.

Non-hierarchical systems
A non-hierarchical structural system consists of a multitude of identical elements that are interconnected and designed in such a way that upon failure of one element, those adjacent to it can take over its function based on the principle of redundancy. In contrast to the hierarchical system, forces are not grouped together here but are spread like a net so that in the event of a local failure they can flow around any damaged or weakened components (Fig. 3). As non-hierarchical loadbearing systems are frequently hyperstatic to a considerable degree (i.e. contain many redundant members), complicated calculations are required to design the components. In addition, such systems react more sensitively to restraint stresses due to thermal loads and deformations.

Loadbearing elements
Planning with glass depends on the maximum available dimensions of the respective primary and secondary glass products as well as the physical properties of the material itself. Furthermore, transport, installation and the replacement of damaged panes are all factors that may govern the dimensions that can be used.

Sheet glass as a basic product
Currently, glass elements cannot be joined together as easily as other building materials. Screwed, bolted and clamped connections represent weak spots within an assembly of components because they cause local stress concentrations that cannot be accommodated by the

glass through ductile behaviour. And, in the case of glued or laminated bonds, there is the risk of creep under permanent loads. In addition, the loading capacity of a glass component is basically very much dependent on its surface quality and edge working. As the float glass method provides us with a cost-effective, high-quality product, two-dimensional sheet glass is favoured as the basic product for structural tasks (p. 43, Fig. 5). It can be cut, shaped or combined with other planar components in such a way that one- and three-dimensional components can be produced.

Typology
Constructional elements can be conveniently classified according to their development in space. We distinguish between one-dimensional (linear) components, two-dimensional (planar) structures and three-dimensional (space) structures. The allocation is carried out by way of the respective slenderness ratio. Apart from that, construction elements can be classified according to their loadbearing function (Fig. 4). As in practice different types of actions cannot always be unequivocally separated, the following breakdown into linear members, planar elements and components with a three-dimensional loadbearing structure is based on the dominant loadbearing function.

If the spatial development of a component in one dimension is considerably greater than that in the other two, it is considered as a one-dimensional component, a linear member. Linear members are further subdivided into columns, beams, posts and fins.

A column is a linear loadbearing element that is primarily loaded in compression. Columns therefore normally have an axially or rotationally symmetrical cross-section

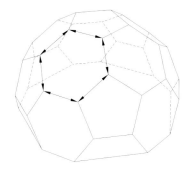

3

made up of pieces of sheet glass or glass tubes. As columns are traditionally primary loadbearing elements in hierarchical structural systems, they play only a minor role in glass constructions. But if glass columns are required, they must be connected top and bottom via pinned joints to ensure that they remain essentially free from any moments (p. 43, Figs. 5 and 6)
A beam is a linear member that is used primarily as a horizontal element loaded in bending. Below, we distinguish between horizontal, inclined and vertical installation positions in a similar way to the Technical Rules for the Use of Glazing on Linear Supports (TRLV) (p. 43, Fig. 8).
Vertical beams are called posts and fins when they carry bending loads in addition to axial loads due to their self-weight. In glass constructions they are mainly used to resist wind loads and reduce the risk of buckling of panes. Very flat posts are normally called fins and are frequently in the form of solid metal sections or laminated safety glass.

Planar elements
A plate is a planar, flat, rigid component loaded only by forces acting in the plane of the plate. A plate can be in the form of a widened column or a very deep beam, and in the form of a shear diaphragm can provide a stiffening or bracing function (Fig. 4). A slab, like a plate, is a planar element, but instead is loaded in bending by external forces caused by loads acting perpendicular to the plane of the system. Those loads include:
· Self-weight
· Snow and wind loads
· Temperature differences on the surfaces
· Displacement of the supports
· Eccentric prestressing forces
In the case of horizontal glazing or sloping glazing at a shallow angle, glass primarily carries out of-of-plane loads, i.e. acts as a slab.

Components with a three-dimensional loadbearing structure
The combination of planar components results in spatial structures whose edges are linked via shear-resistant connections – so-called folded plates. The planar loadbearing components either carry purely in-plane loads or can be loaded in bending.

A three-dimensional, rigid loadbearing structure in single or double curvature is called a shell. Shell-type loadbearing elements can be created through the hot- or cold-working of sheet glass (p. 42, Fig. 4). Besides components made from float glass, pressed glass blocks can also be used for structural purposes in walls or as glazing carrying foot or vehicular traffic.

1 View of the non-hierarchical loadbearing system of a glass geodesic dome; Selimiye Mosque, Haarlem (NL), 2006, De Architectenkamer, Octatube Delft (engineers)
2 Post-and-rail facade: hierarchical facade and roof structure to a cinema entrance foyer; Ufa-Kino, Dresden (D), 1998, Coop Himmelb(l)au
3 Sketch of the principle of the flow of forces in a non-hierarchical loadbearing system in the case of failure of a component using the example of a geodesic dome
4 Typology of prevailing loadbearing, support, force-transfer and component types in glass construction

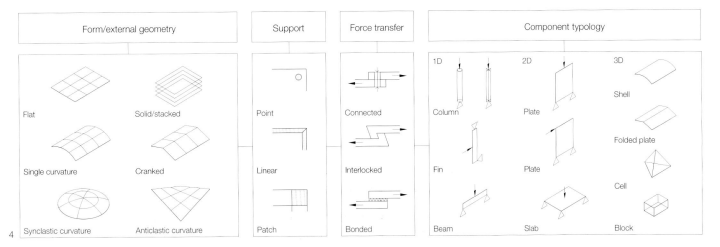

Form/external geometry		Support	Force transfer	Component typology		
Flat	Solid/stacked	Point	Connected	1D Column	2D Plate	3D Shell
Single curvature	Cranked	Linear	Interlocked	Fin	Plate	Folded plate
Synclastic curvature	Anticlastic curvature	Patch	Bonded	Beam	Slab	Cell / Block

4

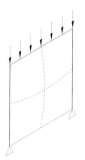

1   Local buckling   Global buckling   Torsional-flexural buckling

Stability, stiffness

Linear and planar loadbearing structures tend to buckle in the direction of their weak axis/axes when subjected to compression and bending loads. This behaviour is known as local, global or torsional-flexural buckling depending on the geometry of the component and the nature and magnitude of the actions involved (Fig. 1). The onset of failure is marked by the available strength being exceeded by the tensile stresses due to flexural tension or transverse bending strains.

If the nature and magnitude of the actions cannot be changed within a loadbearing structure through redesign, appropriate measures must be taken at the level of the building component in order to guarantee stability. The following stiffening options are available in principle: prestressing and the geometrical modification of the component cross-section using the same or a different material.

Modifying the permissible loads
Glass can be modified through controlled cooling in such a way that an inherent compressive stress is induced in the outer surfaces (see "Basic glass and derived products", pp. 16–18). This process increases the tensile bending strength because the inherent compressive stresses must first be overcome before tensile stresses occur. The optical properties of the pane of glass are hardly altered by this secondary treatment. The same effect can be achieved by applying an external prestress: a different material, one with a high level of tensile strength such as steel, is added in such a way that primarily compressive stresses occur within the glass (Figs. 3 and 6).

Modifying the component geometry
On the spatial-geometrical level, it would seem reasonable to increase the structural depth of the weak axis/axes in order to improve the stiffness. This can be achieved with glass as well as with other materials. One possibility is to bond several parallel panes by means of a (transparent) plastic film. Although this increases the toning of the glass and means that the visible edge of the component is wider, it does, however, augment the redundancy and the residual loadbearing capacity. One typical approach is to attach stiffeners, beams and fins in the direction of buckling. The linking of several panes with shear-resistant connections to form a folded plate is another effective solution, likewise the shaping of panes of glass to form shells. Planar sandwich elements consisting of individual panes linked via shear-resistant connections, or T- or I-sections borrowed from structural steelwork, can be produced in glass by employing various methods of connection, and used very effectively. Furthermore, many other conventional materials and techniques can be used with glass to create composite constructions (p. 71, Fig. 6).

1 Possible forms of stability failure in slender building components subjected to compression
2 Stacks of glass panes bonded together form the solid internal and external walls of this private house; Laminata House, Leerdam (NL), 2001, Kruunenberg van der Erve Architekten
3 Externally prestressed glass tubes, with pinned end connections, transfer the horizontal loads on the glass facade back to the row of steel columns behind in this foyer; Tower Place, London (GB), 2002, Foster + Partners
4 Interior view of a hot-worked corrugated glass facade; Casa da Música, Porto (P), 2005, OMA

5

6

Applications

The typical applications and uses of glass in buildings place characteristic demands on the load-carrying capacity of the respective product and its supporting construction. The existing codes of practice and directives are therefore characterised by the loading cases and risks to be expected in conjunction with these. When using glass as a construction material, we distinguish between glazing for vertical, safety barrier, overhead and trafficable (occasional or constant foot traffic) applications.

Vertical glazing

The Technical Rules for the Use of Glazing on Linear Supports (TRLV) make a fundamental distinction between vertical and overhead glazing. In this case, the angle between the plane of the glazing system and a vertical line is critical: up to a maximum of 10° from the vertical, the glazing can be regarded as vertical, but any angle greater than this means that the system must be classed as overhead glazing (Fig. 8). This classification is based on the loads to be expected with such types of glazing (because of the angle). However, if loads – e.g. those caused by snow accumulations on sawtooth roofs – can occur on vertical glazing that are not only brief and transient such as those arising from wind, the provisions for overhead glazing apply. According to the Model List of Technical Construction Regulations, vertical glazing whose top edge is no more than 4 m above a circulation zone (e.g. display windows) is exempted from the TRLV stipulations.

The glass curtain walls of modern office buildings represent a typical vertical glazing application. Situated at the interface between interior and exterior, they have to satisfy numerous, sometimes conflicting, requirements: on the one hand they have

to function as a climate, energy and acoustic barrier, and on the other, provide controlled permeability for light, air and heat. In addition, they may also have to protect against fire, intruders, bullets or explosions, and maybe prevent persons falling from a higher to a lower level. The use of large areas of transparent glass panes is indispensable for ensuring adequate admission of daylight and a view of the outside world (a legal requirement). As the maximum height of the glazing exerts a great influence on the supply of daylight to areas further back within the building, glass facades often extend the full height of a storey. Glass used in a facade can form part of the tertiary structure, i.e. perform purely infilling tasks, or act as a structural member as part of the secondary or even the primary loadbearing system.

Carrying the loads
The facade is frequently divided into structurally effective components that are specifically planned for resisting the vertical or horizontal components of the following loads:
• Self-weight
• Snow loads
• Wind loads
• Imposed loads
• Impact loads (see pp. 46–48)
• Loads due to restraint forces resulting from thermal loads, settlement, explosions, earthquakes, etc.

In principle, there are two practical ways in which facades can be designed to carry loads:
A "suspended construction" is supported from the floor above each storey so that the self-weight of the facade causes tensile forces within the material. This arrangement overcomes stability problems. However, strength problems can occur at the suspension points due to stress concentrations.

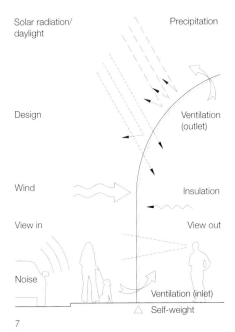

7

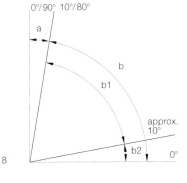

8

5   Loadbearing glass column in a café and bar in Göppingen (D), 2003, Mario Hägele, Attila Acs
6   Externally prestressed glass column in a private house, Planungsgruppe MDP, 2003
7   Overview of the complex requirements placed on windows and glass facades
8   Classification of types of glazing according to its angle with the vertical
    a Vertical glazing
    b Overhead glazing
      b1 Sloping glazing
      b2 Horizontal glazing

| Post-and-rail construction | Posts only | Trusses | Rails with cables | Cable-stayed facade | Parallel cables |

    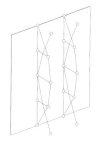 

1

2

3

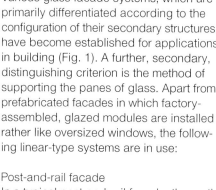

4

A "standing construction", on the other hand, is supported on the floor below and transfers the vertical loads occurring to the primary structure by way of compression. Without suitable bracing measures, such a form of construction may suffer from stability problems.

Facade systems
Various glass facade systems, which are primarily differentiated according to the configuration of their secondary structures, have become established for applications in building (Fig. 1). A further, secondary, distinguishing criterion is the method of supporting the panes of glass. Apart from prefabricated facades in which factory-assembled, glazed modules are installed rather like oversized windows, the following linear-type systems are in use:

Post-and-rail facade
In a typical post-and-rail facade, the vertical posts and horizontal rails form a grid of square or rectangular bays (p. 40, Fig. 2). The cross-sectional sizes of the posts and rails are frequently different from each other; however, their surfaces in contact with the glass are generally flush so that the panes can be supported on all four sides. The edges of the glass are normally clamped in place by patent glazing bars concealed, in turn, behind capping strips. A multitude of standardised systems is available on the market for this popular type of facade construction.

Posts-only facade
The glass in this type of facade is supported on vertical beams, normally clamped along two sides or held by point supports. The secondary structure supports the self-weight of the facade and resists wind loads. A permanently resilient sealing material seals the visible butt joints. All manner of construction forms may be used for the vertical beams

– from simple hollow steel sections to trusses and trussed arrangements. The omission of the horizontal rails can help to increase the degree of transparency of a facade compared to a post-and-rail design, which is why a posts-only facade is frequently favoured for architectural reasons (Fig. 2).

Rails-only facade
In this type of facade, horizontal beams resist the horizontal loads acting on the facade. The vertical facade loads are frequently transferred to the suspended floors via vertical ties attached to the rails (see "Case studies", Production building in Hettenhausen, pp. 90–91). The rails divide the facade horizontally, and this effect can be emphasized by placing the longer side of the glass planes horizontally as well.

Structural sealant glazing (SSG)
This is a form of construction in which the glass is bonded to the supporting construction with adhesive instead of being clamped or screwed. A silicone adhesive functions as both the loadbearing and sealing element in this solution. Such facades are characterised by a smooth, contourless outer skin defined only by the pattern of adhesive joints (Fig. 3, see also "Constructing with glass", pp. 68–71).

Cable facade
Such facades are designed as suspended constructions so that tensile forces are primarily generated, thus enabling a delicate form of construction. Grids of horizontal and vertical prestressed cables (cable nets) are common. In the case of cable-stayed facades, special bracing cables resist the horizontal loads. In contrast to this, there are also systems of parallel cables that can only accommodate the vertical forces through controlled deflection of the facade (Fig. 4). In both types of

construction, the panes of glass are normally supported at individual points. There are especially ambitious cable structures that exploit the relatively high compressive strength of the glass in the overall facade design; however, they are not covered by any standards.

All-glass facade

All-glass facades are mostly designed as suspended constructions. Glass fins, connected to the panes of glass via mechanical fasteners or adhesive, can be added to provide horizontal stiffening. The individual components carry the vertical loads. In principle, all-glass facades can be designed as very elegant standing constructions. The panes of glass enclosing the interior can, at the same time, resist wind loads acting perpendicular to the plane of the system, accommodate shear forces in the plane of the glass and even support the axial forces due to additional components, e.g. a roof. This means that primary, secondary and tertiary structures are all combined in one component. However, owing to the aforementioned risks that always accompany the use of glass, such facades are normally used only for small single-storey buildings not open to the public, e.g. pavilions or private houses (Fig. 5).

1 Typology of customary facade systems
2 Post-only facade in the foyer of the refurbished local government building in Münster (Westphalia) (D), 2006, Kresing Architekten
3 Example of a structural sealant glazing (SSG) facade; Main Tower, Frankfurt am Main (D), 2001, ASP Schweger Assoziierte
4 Cable facade, University of Bremen (D), 2002, Alsop & Störmer Architects, seele GmbH & Co. KG (engineers)
5 Loadbearing glass facade to a private house, Klein Residence, Santa Fe, New Mexico (USA), 2004, Ohlhausen DuBois Architects

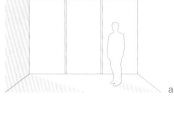

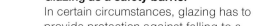

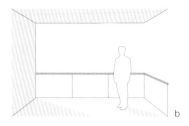

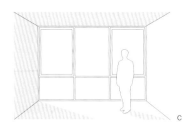

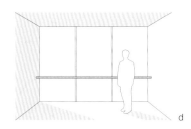

Glazing as a safety barrier

In certain circumstances, glazing has to provide protection against falling to a lower level. Germany's Model Building Code (MBO) stipulates that constructions with a height of fall of > 1 m must be provided with protective barriers on all sides. For example, rooflights not designed for foot traffic, stairs, roofs and floor openings must be reliably protected. A balustrade height of 0.9 m (or 0.8 m in the case of a spandrel panel) is required up to heights of 12 m, and 1.1 m above that. The methods of calculation and component testing are based on the scenario of a person deliberately or accidentally colliding with a vertical glazing element. These elements must be designed in such a way that they can prevent a person falling to a lower level in addition to withstanding the effects of self-weight, wind, climate and normal horizontal imposed loads. In the case of breakage, the fragments of glass should be blunt in order to minimise the risk of injuries. And broken pieces of glass on the outer face should not be able to fall onto circulation zones below. Furthermore, the glazing should offer sufficient resistance to penetration.

Design guidelines
In Germany the Technical Rules for Glass in Safety Barriers (TRAV) document provides planning aids for constructions that have been verified in theory and tried and tested in practice. With their help, designers and contractors can devise constructions that can be built rapidly, are reliable in terms of building technology and relatively cost-effective. Solutions that comply fully or to a large degree with the recommendations given in the TRAV will not have to undergo any further (costly and time-consuming) testing. Verification is carried out in two steps: firstly, "proof of loadbearing capacity under static actions" must be established by calculation, as is the case for glazing not subject to any special requirements; secondly, "proof of loadbearing capacity

1 Interior view of glazing also serving as a safety barrier according to TRAV category A; meeting room, CUBE services centre, Münster (D), 2007, GOP Architekten & Kaufleute
2 Categories of safety barrier glazing according to the TRAV:
  a Category A: vertical glazing with linear supports but without structural rail at height required by building regulations
  b Category B: glass balustrade fully fixed at the base along its entire length, with continuous handrail
  c Category C2: vertical glazing with linear supports on at least two opposite sides located below a structural transverse rail at handrail height
  d Category C3: category A glazing behind a structural transverse rail
3 According to the TRAV, glass edges are regarded as protected when their distance to neighbouring components measured in the plane of the glass is no greater than 30 mm. Balustrade infill panels of laminated safety glass with fixings in drilled holes are exempted from this requirement.
4 Facade with cantilevering glazed meeting cubes, CUBE services centre, Münster (D), 2007, GOP Architekten & Kaufleute

≤ 30 mm   ≤ 30 mm

under impact-type actions" must be checked (see "Building legislation provisions", pp. 76–80). The TRAV covers the following situations:

- Vertical glazing that must also prevent a fall to a lower level
- Loadbearing glass spandrel panels with a continuous handrail
- Balustrade infill panels of glass

The exemption for glazing elements whose top edge is max. 4 m above a circulation zone does not apply here. Safety barrier glazing is divided into three categories according to the requirements it has to meet:

Category A:
This category covers glazing with linear supports in the meaning of the TRLV provisions but no loadbearing rail or handrail on the room side of the glass to withstand horizontal loads at the height prescribed by building regulations (Fig. 2a). The edges of the glazing must be reliably protected against impacts, either by the supports (e.g. posts, rails, adjacent panes) or directly adjacent components (e.g. walls, floors). A typical example of category A glazing is full-height windows to the facades of office buildings. Vertical glazing on top of a spandrel panel whose height does not comply with the building regulations also falls within this category. This is also the case with windows near floor level and glazed doors where there are no additional safety barriers on the outside. As glass itself forms the safety barrier, single glazing must be made from laminated safety glass. In the case of multi-pane insulating glass, combinations of laminated safety glass and other products are permitted (see p. 62, Tab. T2).

Category B
This category covers loadbearing glass balustrades with linear supports, the individual panes of which are interconnected by means of a handrail enclosing the top

edge (Fig. 2b). The glazing must consist of single glazing made from laminated safety glass, the bottom edge of which is fully fixed. The handrail, besides protecting the top edge of the glass balustrade, must also withstand the design horizontal loads possible at that height should any one of the glass elements fail (redundancy principle). Such handrails are therefore in the form of a loadbearing channel section with a non-loadbearing cap (as the actual handrail) or a loadbearing metal handrail with an integral channel section; both variants are bonded securely to the top of the glass balustrade. At each end, the handrail is normally connected to a post or wall so that the loads on the handrail can still be safely resisted should the end bay of glass fail.

The TRAV recommends a form of construction for this category (Fig. 5). The panes of glass may also be clamped by some other sufficiently stiff form of mounting construction. However, if, as shown, the glass has to be drilled to accommodate bolts or screws, the use of laminated safety glass made from toughened safety or heat-strengthened glass is recommended because in the case of non-toughened glass the zone around the drilled hole has a much lower strength than the rest of the pane.

Unsupported edges of balustrade infill panels of glass must always be protected against damage. According to the TRAV, such edges are regarded as protected when the clear distance from the edge of the glass to the next pane of glass or other adjacent component does not exceed 30 mm in the plane of the glass (Fig. 3). This requirement does not apply to glass infill panels made from laminated safety glass and supported by way of fixings in drilled holes because such panes of glass remain in place even after failure.

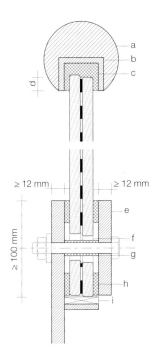

5

5 Example of the construction principle for a glass safety barrier according to TRAV category B
   a Handrail
   b Loadbearing channel section
   c Elastomeric strip and filling of sealant to DIN 18545-2 group E
   d Edge cover in channel section ≥ 15 mm
   e Steel clamping plate min. 12 mm thick
   f Drilled hole in glass aligned with centre of clamping plate, 25 mm ≤ d ≤ 35 mm
   g Plastic sleeve
   h Bearing pad of rigid elastomer, continuous in longitudinal direction
   i Setting block

a

b

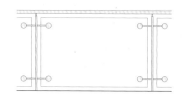

c

1d

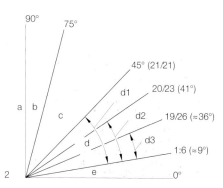

2

Category C
This category covers infill glazing that acts as a safety barrier but where the horizontal loads are resisted by another component. The category is divided into three groups depending on the particular form of construction:

Group C1 covers balustrade infill panels with point and/or linear supports on at least two opposite sides (Fig. 1). Apart from the instance of support on all sides, laminated safety glass is mandatory. Point-supported glazing is only permitted for flat, square/rectangular panes of glass in interior applications. The point supports can be in the form of fixings in drilled holes (Fig. 1d) or clamp fittings (Fig. 1c). The reliability of the latter type of support is, however, difficult to achieve and verify because the PVB interlayer of laminated safety glass tends to creep under permanent loading and the glass could slip out of its fixing (see "Constructing with glass", p. 63).

According to the TRAV, Group C2 covers vertical glazing with linear supports on at least two opposite sides below a load-resisting transverse rail at handrail height (p. 46, Fig. 2c). For example, this applies to post-and-rail constructions or windows with a fixed glass spandrel panel element.

Group C3 covers category A glazing with a load-resisting handrail on the room side at the height required by the building regulations (p. 46, Fig. 2d).

Deviations from the square/rectangular form
Glazed safety barriers along the edges of floors frequently join directly with staircase balustrades. In order that the same materials and design can be used for both – and thus create a consistent appearance –

without having to carry out impact tests, the TRAV permits deviations from square or rectangular panes of glass. Such panes may be transformed into parallelograms whose top and bottom edges form an angle not exceeding 41° measured from a horizontal plane. This angle corresponds to the maximum permissible pitch (200 mm rise, 230 mm going) for "stairs required by building regulations that lead to habitable rooms in residential buildings with no more than two dwellings" according to DIN 18065 "Stairs in buildings" (Fig. 2). In practice it is therefore possible to use glass safety barriers for many typical applications without having to carry out costly, time-consuming impact tests. However, other forms such as triangles, ovals and special shapes that deviate from a parallelogram (e.g. at top/bottom of stairs) will require separate verification.

1 Category C1 glazing: balustrade infill panel with point and/or linear supports on at least two opposite sides:
   a Glazing with linear supports on both vertical sides
   b Glazing with linear supports top and bottom
   c Glazing with point supports in the form of clamping plates
   d Glazing with point supports in drilled holes
2 Definition of ramps, stairs and ladders to DIN 18065:
   a Step irons
   b Ladders
   c Stepladders
   d Stairs
      d1 Basement and attic access stairs that do not lead to habitable rooms, also (additional) stairs not required by building regulations
      d2 Stairs required by building regulations that lead to habitable rooms in residential buildings with no more than two dwellings
      d3 Stairs required by building regulations in non-residential buildings
   e Ramps

3

4

Overhead glazing

According to the TRLV, overhead glazing is any glazing at an angle of more than 10° to the vertical (p. 43, Fig. 8); exceptions according to the Model List of Technical Construction Regulations are Velux-type roof windows in dwellings and rooms with similar uses having an unobstructed glazed area not exceeding 1.6 m² and glazing to glasshouses. The technical rules are based on the nature and magnitude of the loads to be expected plus the risks that such a form of construction involves. In contrast to vertical glazing, which is primarily loaded by its own weight in the plane of the system, as the angle between the overhead glazing and the vertical increases, the force component that acts permanently perpendicular to the plane of the glass increases as well. The infilling glass panes are therefore increasingly subjected to bending and act more and more like a slab instead of a plate. In addition to self-weight, overhead glazing may also have to carry snow loads. And, in contrast to vertical glazing which would normally only have to resist brief loads perpendicular to the plane of the glass (e.g. due to wind), such loads represent long-term actions on overhead glazing. This is why glazing that only slopes at an angle of 10° to the vertical must still be classed as overhead glazing when certain loads are to be expected that exert more than a short-term influence on the glass, e.g. snow accumulations on sawtooth roofs. Furthermore, there are buildings in which vertical glazing gradually changes to overhead glazing (p. 51, Fig. 5). In such cases, the individual segments must be handled according to their angle of inclination; but where maximum homogeneity of the construction is desired, such glazing should be designed according to the more unfavourable case. Curved overhead glazing and glazing that is intended to act as a bracing element are not covered by the rules. Overhead glazing usually requires more design work than vertical glazing. This is due to the tendency to use longer spans, the fact that the loads are perpendicular to the plane of the system and the greater safety risks.

Areas of application

As overhead glazing allows more daylight into an interior than vertical glazing, it is often preferred where a high level of natural daylight and, at the same time, protection from the weather is required. Overhead glazing is frequently the only sensible option when rooms deep within the building need natural illumination. The German Places of Work Directive calls for a visual link with the outside world, but only at eye level by way of windows, glazed doors or transparent wall surfaces. This requirement is therefore met by vertical glazing, and an unobstructed view through overhead glazing is not always necessary. Therefore, many different types of construction are possible in principle.

Modern forms of glass construction – in the form of both autonomous systems and subsystems – are used in new buildings, but also as additions to, or in conjunction with, existing buildings. Due to their seemingly technical architectural language, glass constructions stand out distinctly from existing elements, but their lightweight, dematerialising effect does not overwhelm them. Glass roofs can have a powerful influence on the effect of a space, but can be designed in such a way that they do not alter the underlying character of the original building: transparency allows the existing elements to be perceived and in no way visually curtailed.

5

3   Suspended nets to prevent larger pieces of glass falling onto circulation zone below; New Trade Fair, Leipzig (D), 1995, gmp Architekten von Gerkan, Marg & Partner
4   Suspended glass-and-steel structure; local authority pavilion, Hoofddorp (NL), 2002, Asymptote, Octatube, Delft (engineers)
5   Glass shell with synclastic curvature made from several hot-worked panes of glass and a metal tension ring; loadbearing glass dome at the Institute for Lightweight Structures & Conceptual Design (ILEK), University of Stuttgart (D), 2005, W. Sobek and L. Blandini

1

2

Risks and safety mechanisms
It can be assumed that sloping or horizontal glazing over areas used by people constitutes a higher safety risk than is the case with vertical glazing due to the increased possibility of its being damaged accidentally or deliberately by falling hard objects (Fig. 1). At the same time, there is an increased risk of damage should glazing units, either as a whole or in the form of sharp and heavy broken fragments, fall onto circulation zones. In order to minimise these risks, overhead glass structures must be designed with inherent redundancy and the components used must possess an adequate residual loadbearing capacity and at the same time bond any broken pieces. At component level, the TRLV stipulates that only wired or laminated safety glass made from annealed or heat-strengthened glass may be used for single glazing or the lower pane of insulating glass. It is not possible to use laminated safety glass made from toughened safety glass because this exhibits a poor residual loadbearing capacity (Tab. T1 and Fig. 1). Protection against larger fragments of falling glass can also be achieved by spanning nets below the glass (max. mesh size 40 mm) (p. 49, Fig. 3). Other solutions can also be approved in principle, even though they are not explicitly mentioned in the guidelines and codes of practice, provided they achieve the protective aims through the use of other glass products or other constructional measures,

e.g. attaching a film to protect against splinters.

Typology
As already mentioned in the section "Loadbearing elements" (pp. 40–41), construction elements can be classified according to their external geometry. In the overall loadbearing structure, a differentiation is also made between flat, single curvature and double curvature systems. One also has to decide whether the glazing has to accommodate only those forces that act directly on its surface or whether it also has to contribute to the loadbearing action of the overall construction, i.e. provide a bracing function in addition to its infilling function.

Loadbearing structures in double curvature
Loadbearing structures with double, synclastic curvature can be designed in such a way that the shell effect results in permanent loads to the structural components being principally in the form of axial forces. This makes it possible for these systems to be designed especially elegantly and economically (Fig. 5). However, the building authorities demand relatively high safety margins for glass loadbearing structures, a fact that does not always have a positive effect on the design. Even though there are examples of glass constructions loaded in tension (e.g. in facades), using glass as a material in compression represents a good

T1: Permissible uses of glass products in overhead applications according to the TRLV

		monolithic glass type					Lam. safety glass made from...		
		An-nealed	Tough. safety	Wired	Rolled	Lamin-ated	Annealed	Heat-strength.	Tough. safety
Single glazing				+			+	+	
Insulating glazing Position of pane	top	+	+	+	+	+	+	+	+
	bottom			+			+	+	

Alternative: constructional measures to prevent larger pieces of glass falling onto circulating zones below (e.g. nets with mesh size ≤ 40 mm)

3

4

option for overhead glazing. Although it is not regulated, the use of glass that has been bent to follow the form of the building exactly is particularly appealing. In particular, reflections in large-format facades with curved panes appear considerably more harmonious than those with faceted glazing (Figs. 3 and 5).

Loadbearing structures in single curvature
Thesw structures, so-called barrel vaults, represent another type of construction that, in principle, is suitable for glass. Here, the panes of glass can be used not only as part of the building envelope, but also as part of the loadbearing structure (Fig. 3). The use of single, bent panes can be worthwhile for shorter spans (Fig. 2).

Plane systems
When loadbearing structures are flat or have only a very minor curvature and are supported in such a way that they are mainly subjected to bending, we speak of plane systems. Such systems are used, for example, when the overall depth available is limited or the horizontal forces that would ensue from an arch-type construction could not be safely transferred to the supporting structure or resisted by ties.

Apart from that, plane systems often represent a cost-effective solution thanks to their simpler planning processes and modular components. Generally, we can expect systems loaded primarily in bending to require more materials than those with the same boundary conditions but primarily subjected to axial forces, a fact that can influence the appearance and degree of transparency. Grids of metal or timber sections typically form the supporting framework to overhead glazing. One special variant, however, is the plane all-glass system in which the elements form the secondary structure. The bending stresses that occur under permanent loads, the relatively low tensile bending strength of glass products and the transferring of moments to adjacent components must be given special attention. Whereas float glass is available in standard lengths up to 6 m, the dimensions of the autoclaves in which laminated safety glasses are produced generally only permit smaller sizes. In order to span longer distances with glass, it is usually necessary to join several elements together. But, as rigid glass-to-glass connections are difficult to produce because they cause stress concentrations at the con-

nection points, alternative solutions are frequently chosen. The construction of the glass roof to the Apple Store on New York's 5th Avenue is based on traditional Chinese loadbearing concepts for bridges and roofs (p. 52, Figs. 3, 4 and 5). The glass roof consists of an orthogonal, non-hierarchical system of glass beams connected exclusively by means of pinned joints. In this orthogonal arrangement, the forces from two adjacent beams are always introduced at the middle of each beam. A similar structural concept was used for the canopy to an underground station entrance in Tokyo (p. 52, Fig. 2). In this case, parallel, pin-jointed glass lamellae form cantilever beams on which the glazing has been laid. The beams consist of glass and transparent plastic sheets. Their thickness increases towards the support, corresponding to the flow of forces.

1   Laminated safety glass in which all the laminations are made from toughened safety glass is not permissible in many applications, e.g. overhead glazing, because once all the laminations are broken it has no residual loadbearing capacity and simply collapses.
2   Patented roofing system consisting of cold-worked curved glazing and steel ties. It forms a self-contained structure in itself and therefore can be mounted on any suitable supporting construction. If a glazing unit fails, it is intercepted by the ties and hence prevented from falling to the floor. Central bus terminal, Heidenheim (D), 2003, Molenaer Architekten
3   Roof over an internal courtyard in the form of a glass barrel vault. Whereas the compression forces that occur flow through the glazing, the steel bracing cables form shear diaphragms. Guy cables ensure that the overall construction is divided into segments. Maximilian Museum, Augsburg (D), 1999, Augsburg Building Department, Ludwig & Weiler Ingenieure (now: Tragkonzept)
4   Trussed flat glass roof over castle ruins; Juval Castle, South Tyrol (I), 1997, Robert Danz
5   Cold-worked, long panes of glass form the smooth outer shell to the entrance foyer of Strasbourg Central Station (F), 2007, AREP, RFR (engineers)

5

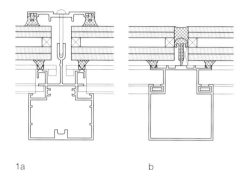

1a   b

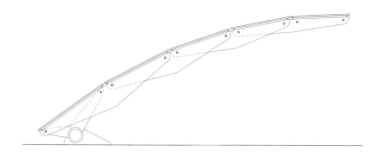

2

Also conceivable are systems in which the plane of the glazing not only forms the building envelope and is supported on some type of framing, but also constitutes the top chord of a trussed system and as such accommodates the compression forces. Only a few such examples have been built to date; some of them only experiments as part of ongoing research projects (see "Building legislation provisions", p. 80, Fig. 1).

Special constructional aspects for sloping and horizontal glazing
On the constructional level, we distinguish between sloping and horizontal glazing depending on the angle of inclination to the horizontal (p. 43, Fig. 8, b1 and b2). It is not possible to use conventional patent glazing bars in the transverse direction below an angle of about 10° to the horizontal because they can hinder water run-off. In addition, shallow angles severely hamper the self-cleaning function of the

glass. In the case of truly horizontal glazing, not all the water can drain off and the deflection of the panes of glass due to their self-weight makes ponding unavoidable; a minimum fall of 2 % is therefore advisable. Special transverse glazing bars flattened on the upward side can be used to improve the water run-off. If it is not possible to use such glazing bars, it is better to omit them completely, support the panes on two sides only and seal the transverse joints with silicone (Fig. 1).

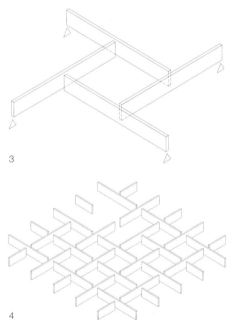

3

4

5

1   Horizontal sections through roof glazing
    a Parallel to direction of fall
    b Transverse to direction of fall
    Government offices, St. Germain-en-Laye (F),
    1994, Brunet Saunier
2   Section through glass canopy cantilevering
    approx. 9 m; Tokyo International Forum (J), 1996,
    Rafael Vinoly, Dewhurst Macfarlane & Partners
    (engineers)
3, 4 Loadbearing concept for a glass roof;
    Apple Store, 5th Avenue, New York (USA), 2006,
    Bohlin Cywinski Jackson, Eckersley O'Callaghan
    (engineers)
5   External view of the Apple Store

6

Glazing for foot traffic

Wherever transparency and a particular redirection of the light are important, glazed building components would seem to be the obvious option. Trafficable glazing is fully accessible to the users of a building and designed to be walked on. As such traffic loads are generally additional to the normal loads on overhead glazing, the construction must satisfy both requirements.
Typical areas of application are:
• Stairs
• Landings
• Galleries
• Walkways
• Roofs over lightwells
• Glass bridges
• Glass roofs

Glazing for foot traffic can be designed for both indoor and outdoor applications, but in Germany a national technical approval (AbZ) or an individual approval (ZiE) will always be required. Exceptions are steps or landing elements that cannot be accessed by vehicular traffic and are not subject to high permanent loads or a high risk of impacts. According to the TRLV these should be designed as glazing units with continuous linear supports on all sides. The TRLV specifies three panes of laminated safety glass as a minimum for trafficable glazing. However, the topmost pane, of heat-strengthened glass at least 10 mm thick, may not be taken into account when designing the load-carrying capacity of the glazing because it will be subjected to severe mechanical damage. The scratches and cracks that are inevitable reduce the loadbearing capacity of the uppermost pane considerably and it should be regarded as a wearing course only. Each of the two panes underneath must be of annealed or heat-strengthened glass at least 12 mm thick (Fig. 7). Furthermore,

the dimensions are limited to 400 × 1500 mm and a glass edge cover of a minimum of 30 mm is necessary. As only glazing supported on all sides is covered by the regulations, this restriction results in the glass surface being fitted into some kind of frame. In the case of steps in particular, which tend to be rather narrow components, the minimum edge cover has a negative effect on the light permeability. This means that aesthetically interesting glass stair constructions, while possible, are usually outside the scope of standardised forms of construction.

Of course, aspects of stability and serviceability must be proved by calculation in addition to taking into account the constructional details according to the TRLV. Trafficable glazing and its supporting construction must satisfy the same structural requirements as other components made from other materials according to DIN 1055-3 "Actions on structures – Part 3: Self-weight and imposed loads in building". But owing to the brittle failure behaviour of glass, proof of local minimum loadbearing capacity must be provided as well. This is verified using the loading case of self-weight plus a point load applied at the most unfavourable position; whether a 1.5 or 2.0 kN point load is used depends on the magnitude of the imposed load relevant for design.

A number of other aspects should be considered when planning trafficable glazing. Persons can feel uneasy when walking on a completely transparent floor; this psychological effect can be counteracted by reducing the transparency, e.g. by way of printing or a matt finish. Furthermore, care should be taken to ensure that transparent building components do not enable any indiscreet glimpses;

transparent, trafficable overhead glazing is especially affected by this aspect. And the client, or in Germany the employers' liability insurance association concerned, can also demand the provision of a non-slip floor finish, as required by safety regulations. The degree of non-slip finish is determined according to DIN 51130 "Testing of floor coverings – Determination of the anti-slip properties" as follows: a person wearing standardised footwear walks upright backwards and forwards on a floor covering smeared with a lubricant; the surface is gradually raised from the horizontal and the angle of inclination

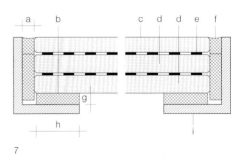

7

6 Underside of glazing designed for foot traffic; Apple Store, Regent Street, London (GB), 2004, Bohlin Cywinski Jackson, Eckersley O'Callaghan (engineers)
7 Typical configuration and support for glazing designed for foot traffic according to the TRLV
   a ≥ 8 mm
   b Elastomeric, e.g. silicone, bearing pad, Shore A hardness 60–80
   c Wearing pane of min. 10 mm toughened safety or heat-strengthened glass, non-slip finish
   d Annealed or heat-strengthened glass, min. 12 mm
   e PVB interlayer, min. 1.52 mm
   f Seal, e.g. silicone DC 993
   g Depth of pad 5–10 mm
   h Edge cover min. 30 mm (for a span of max. 400 mm: 20 mm)
   i Supporting construction

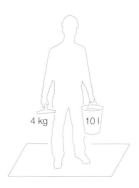

1

2

3

4

at which it is no longer possible to walk safely, the so-called acceptance angle, governs the allocation to one of five groups, R9 (roughest) to R13 (smoothest). Although dry float glass exhibits quite good non-slip properties, the friction decreases considerably once the glass is wet. There are several ways of influencing the surface roughness of sheet glass:

• Sand-blasting
• Mechanical treatment (e.g. milling)
• Laser treatment
• Etching with hydrofluoric acid
• Printing with a non-slip coating

There are, however, conflicts of interest between the non-slip, cleaning and durability requirements. Whereas surfaces treated with "subtractive" methods, such as sand-blasting or etching, are very difficult to clean, "additive" ceramic-ink printing is vulnerable to wear. In order to prevent stumbling, the non-slip characteristics of adjacent surfaces should not differ significantly. There is legal uncertainty as to which surfaces should belong to which non-slip group, and the requirements should be agreed with the client or the future users of the building at an early stage.

Glazing for limited foot traffic

In contrast to trafficable glazing accessible to the general public, there are glass surfaces that only serve as temporary working places and access routes for the purposes of inspection and maintenance. During the design stage, it is important to establish whether the circulation zones below such glazing can be cordoned off for the duration of inspection or maintenance work. If this is possible, then "no building legislation requirements result from the accessibility" [5] and the approval of the senior building authority is unnecessary. However, industrial

safety regulations may call for additional safety measures such as the wearing of safety harnesses. According to DIN 4426 "Equipment for building maintenance – Safety requirements for workplaces and access", measures to prevent sliding off a smooth surface are already necessary at a roof pitch of just 5°. And at pitches exceeding 20°, additional requirements must be complied with.

If it is not possible to cordon off the area below the glazing, the area designed for limited foot traffic must be treated like overhead glazing that must satisfy additional requirements. Persons required to walk on such glazing must be specially instructed. Such surfaces may only be accessed by one person at a time, carrying a single object (e.g. a tool) weighing not more than 4 kg and a 10 l plastic bucket filled with water (Fig. 1). Tests on building components are based on this scenario [6]. However, a special inspection and maintenance concept can be called for.

1 Maximum permissible load on glazing designed for occasional foot traffic
2 Stairs in the Four Seasons Centre for the Performing Arts, Toronto (CAN), 2006, Diamond + Schmitt, Halcrow Yolles
3 Glass spiral stairs; Apple Store, 5th Avenue, New York (USA), 2006, Bohlin Cywinski Jackson, seele GmbH & Co. KG, Eckersley O'Callaghan (engineers)
4 Rooflight designed to accept foot traffic; museum, Denver (USA), 2007, Adjaye
5 This glass wall is readily visible thanks to printing, plastic sheets, etc; SureStart on the Ocean, London (GB), 2007, muf architecture/art
6 Sample of bird protection glazing with special coating

5

6

Safety of glass in circulation zones

Transparent and highly reflective components or buildings in or bordering on public areas harbour particular risks for people and animals. Children, sportspersons and people with mobility or visual impairments are particularly at risk. In principle, two approaches can be applied to minimise the safety risks arising from glass building components: reducing the probability of accidental impact by means of suitable measures (active safety), or designing the components in such a way that serious injuries are unlikely in the case of an accident (passive safety). In Germany, the legal obligation to take appropriate measures is derived from various sources, in particular the building regulations of the federal states. Apart from that, depending on the specific situation, there are statutory instruments, standards and directives, e.g. DIN standards, workplace acts/ directives, safety regulations and the advisory documents of accident insurers, that may need to be complied with.

Measures for reducing the risk of accidental impact

There are numerous ways of preventing people or vehicles colliding accidentally with glass components. One option is to separate the glass construction from the adjacent circulation route by way of barriers, physically or visually. Outdoors, the provision of peripheral bollards, flower beds, hedges, strips of grass or pools represents potential solutions. Indoors, balustrades fixed in the vicinity of a facade, handrails or spandrel panels in front of glass elements are space-saving solutions (see pp. 46–48). In addition, potential trip hazards should be avoided in the vicinity of glazing. Another aspect to be considered is connected with making glass surfaces discernible; the glazing used in construction is often extremely transparent or higly reflective

and, therefore, difficult to see. In both cases, we perceive either the area behind the glass or a reflection of the side where we are standing. Opaque stickers, printing, transverse rails, balustrades, spandrel panels, matt finishes or tinting can all help to enhance the visibility of glass surfaces. Where it is not possible to exclude deliberate or – despite extensive measures – accidental impacts, security glazing should be used.

The protection of animals is another aspect that should be considered in addition to the protection of persons. Many birds perish either directly or indirectly as a result of colliding with a glass surface because they obviously cannot perceive transparent or highly reflective surfaces. Studies have shown that stationary silhouettes of birds of prey are practically ineffective. Measures to decrease the reflections and transparency of the overall construction, and reduce its attractiveness to birds, should therefore be considered. Panes of glass that distort the view considerably also seem to be suitable. If such measures are not suitable for the architectural concept of the project, specially coated glass that birds can detect easily but is hardly noticeable by humans can be used to reduce this conflict (Fig. 6).

[1] Hecht, 2005, p. 208
[2] Gregory, 2001, p. 115ff.
[3] Ganslandt, 1992, p. 79
[4] Knaack, 1998, p. 13
[5] Baden-Wurttemberg Centre for Building
    Technology, 2008, p. 8
[6] DIN 4426, 2001, 5.1.2, and GS-BAU-18, 2001

Constructing with glass

The considerable knowledge of the material properties of glass that is now available has led to its increasing use as a building component with a safety function. More than with any other building material, the utmost attention must be paid to the use of glass in construction in order to prevent failure due to local stress peaks. This chapter first deals with the main principles of constructing with glass. This is followed by an overview of possible forms of support for glass constructions. Proven fixing forms employing clamping, bolting and bonding techniques are all covered in detail.

Appropriate forms of construction for glass
Using glass as a building material presumes that the idiosyncrasies of this material – above all its susceptibility to local stress peaks and the resulting risk of brittle failure – are taken into account. In order to guarantee adequate loadbearing capacity, glass components are always designed with the maximum permissible tensile strength. This aspect must also be considered when selecting methods of fixing and connection, and designing the details. The arrangement of the glass components and connections within the loadbearing structure determines the nature and magnitude of the actions and stresses.

An arrangement to suit the loads and stresses is particularly important when establishing the design of a glass component. Owing to the brittleness of glass, local stress peaks and unworked, sharp edges should be avoided wherever possible. Moreover, glass accepts compressive loads far better than tensile ones, although, in principle, wide support and force-transfer faces are advantageous.

The valid rules and directives provide information on the best geometries for glass elements. Particular attention should be paid to drilled holes and edge working. Local stress peaks are particularly likely to occur adjacent to drilled holes and cut edges. This can be relevant to the design and hence have an influence on the geometry of the component. Furthermore, unintentional eccentricity at supports and play in drilled holes must be avoided.

The configuration of a glass component should be chosen in such a way that the component can be properly incorporated in the overall loadbearing structure. It should be remembered that, in order to achieve an adequate margin of structural safety, the failure of individual glass components should be considered during the planning process. The chapter "Designing with glass" (pp. 38–41) describes in detail various concepts for integrating glass into the overall loadbearing structure.

Accidental loads, such as unintentional impacts and deformations of the supporting construction, must be taken into account in the design work to the same extent as design aspects such as dead, wind, snow and thermal loads. Suitable measures should always be taken during the design process to ensure that restraint stresses are avoided, reduced or redistributed.

Design and construction inaccuracies can lead to local stress concentrations in components. In the case of glass, this cannot be compensated for by redistributing the stresses, which increases the risk of the material failing.

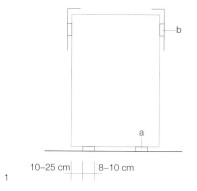

T1: Design principles for building with glass

No contact between glass and harder materials
Avoidance of restraint stresses due to unintentional loads
Choice of a suitable geometry for the glass elements
Specification of a suitable method of connection
Ensuring a sufficient level of robustness of glass constructions
Guarantee of serviceability
Ensuring durability and weather resistance

1

10–25 cm | 8–10 cm

Right   Wrong

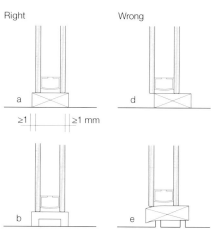

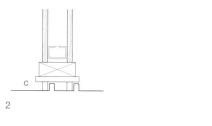

2

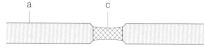

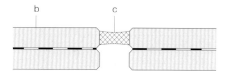

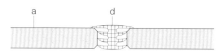

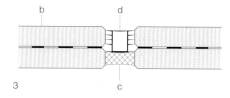

3

The design and detailing must be such that glass does not come into contact with harder materials or damaging mechanical actions. This applies to non-toughened glasses in particular because of their lower strength. Various materials can be used as intermediate pads between glass and harder materials, which also help to absorb any deformations of the supporting construction. Synthetic materials, casting resins or aluminium alloys are especially suitable because they can compensate for small irregularities and ensure a maximum area for the load transfer.

Setting blocks are used to support vertical panes of glass (Figs. 1 and 2). These are pieces of hardwood or plastic that transfer the weight of the glass to the window frame or other supporting construction. DIN 53505 specifies the appropriate Shore hardness depending on the material of the frame. In addition, elastic location blocks made from a synthetic material are inserted in the frame at the sides to help ensure that the panes of glass are supported without any restraint stresses, and, at the same time, prevent direct contact between glass and frame. In the case of a flat-bottomed rebate, bridge packers can be used to ensure vapour pressure equalisation within what would otherwise be an enclosed air space (due to the setting blocks) (Fig. 2b). Packing shims or profiled packers may be needed in the glass rebates to create flat bearing surfaces for setting and location blocks and to adjust the position of the glass vertically (Fig. 2c). All these items must be ageing-resistant, compatible with the adjacent materials, and remain rigid under permanent compression in order to guarantee the functional requirements placed on the window and glazing. Setting blocks are about 80–100 mm long and should be about 2 mm wider than the thickness of

the glass to be supported. They are placed at the bottom edge of the pane, normally 100–250 mm from the corners (Fig. 1). Overhead glazing is treated exactly like vertical glazing in this respect. The weight of each pane must be transferred to the supporting framework via the blocks without overstressing the edges of the glass.

To ensure serviceability, a glass construction must satisfy additional requirements. Besides limits to the deformations, the use of the glass construction must be guaranteed over the lifetime of the building. In terms of building physics requirements, the possibility of condensation, as well as the sealing of joints and cleaning options, must be considered. This means that sealing the joints in glazing elements is a particularly important aspect. As well as providing resistance to the weather, they must act as sound and thermal insulation and be able to absorb various types of induced deformations in order to avoid restraint stresses. Seals to the butt joints between the edges of panes are not usu-

1 Arrangement of setting and location blocks for fixed glazing
  a Setting block
  b Location block
2 Right and wrong setting block positions for insulating glass
  a Setting block positioned correctly
  b Bridge packer positioned correctly
  c Setting block positioned correctly on packing shims in profiled rebate
  d Setting block positioned incorrectly: optimum load distribution is not guaranteed because the insulating glass is not supported across its full thickness.
  e Setting block positioned incorrectly in profiled rebate: the profiling and the weight of the panes deform the setting block such that proper functioning is impossible.
3 Sealing of butt joints by means of sealing compound and/or gasket for monolithic or laminated glass
  a Monolithic glass
  b Laminated (safety) glass
  c Joint sealed with sealing compound
  d Joint sealed with gasket

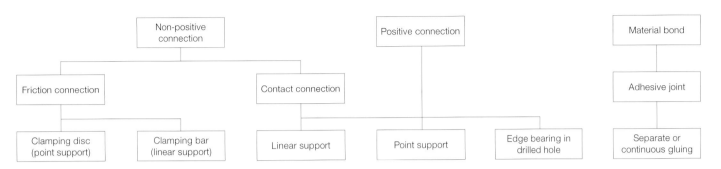

4

ally allocated any loadbearing function. Such joints can be closed with sealing compounds or gaskets or a combination of the two (Fig. 3).
Silicones, polysulphides, polyurethanes and dispersion acrylates are all suitable sealing compounds. By way of adhesion and cohesion forces, these elastic substances compensate for changes in the widths of the joints caused by the changes in position and deformations of adjoining components. The resilience of the seal is determined by the width of the joint and elasticity of the sealant used. In certain circumstances, e.g. a glass shell structure loaded in compression, the sealing materials may also have to provide a structural function.
Gaskets are preformed sealing strips (block or lipped profiles). The necessary degree of sealing is achieved via the contact pressure applied. The displacements of neighbouring panes are accommodated by the lips and lamellae. Such joints should be at least 4 mm thick. Appropriate constructional measures must be employed to protect non-UV-resistant sealing materials against sunlight. Adequate vapour pressure equalisation via openings provided for this purpose prevents condensation at the joints between insulating units. Any water that does collect must be able to drain away via the joints. A movement joint or protection against driving rain can be achieved by overlapping the panes of glass (without contact).

The functionality of a construction can only be guaranteed by using permanently weather-resistant materials. Ultraviolet radiation, pools of water, cleaning agents, and chemical or physical interactions with adjacent materials (galvanic corrosion) should not impair the ageing resistance. In particular, a material's behaviour under permanent loading should be carefully evaluated and tested.

Forms of support in glass constructions
Glass can be employed in many different ways. When using glass as a construction or structural material, we distinguish between vertical and overhead glazing, safety barriers and surfaces intended for constant or occasional foot traffic. Various support options are available for these applications. The methods of securing the glass in position are divided into non-positive, positive and bonded joints (Fig. 4).

In contrast to bonded joints, subsequent detachment is possible with non-positive and positive connections. A non-positive joint is held together by applying a force that presses or clamps the individual parts together. The force transfer is achieved via friction or contact.

In a friction connection the force applied via shear forces (friction) is transferred through the mechanical intermeshing of the contact faces at the joint. Clamping plates (point supports) and bars (linear supports) are used. The intermediate bearing pads are made of soft metals, plastics or other materials; it is their elasticity and durability that determine the quality of the fixing. External forces, moisture or a weakening of the clamping pressure can reduce the friction to such an extent that the panes of glass slip out of their fixings. The compression perpendicular to the contact faces provides the force-transfer mechanism in contact connections. Adequately sized areas for the force transfer and suitable intermediate materials ensure low stresses in the glass in the vicinity of its support. Failure can occur through excessive compression of the materials or by the glass slipping out of its fixing as a result of severe deformations. Positive connections are held together solely via the interlocking geometries of the components.

In a bonded connection the individual components are held together on the atomic and molecular level by the adhesion forces (bonding forces between similar or dissimilar materials) and cohesion forces (internal strength of a substance). Adhesives, welding and soldering are examples of bonded joints. The use of an adhesive enables a force transfer between components that is spread uniformly over a certain area. The thickness and elasticity of the layer of adhesive can minimise local stress concentrations.

4   Types of support for glass constructions

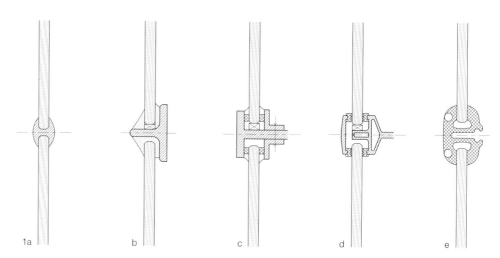

Clamp fixings

A clamp fixing is a combination of a non-positive and positive connection. In the case of vertical glazing, the weight of the glass is carried by the setting blocks. Panes of glass with linear or point supports are generally included among the clamp fixings. Pure friction connections are, for example, clamped safety barriers of category C1 according to the Technical Rules for Glass in Safety Barriers (TRAV). Fig. 2 provides an overview of possible clamp fixings for panes of glass.

Linear-clamped glass without safety barrier function
Leaded lights represent the oldest form of glass with a linear clamped support. Later, glass was fitted into rebates and held in place with glazing sprigs and putty. The clamped support customary today originated from the rebate plus glazing bead (glass placed in frame rebate and wind suction resisted by continuous glazing bead). In this case, the sealing is achieved by an outer an inner seal. The rebate in the frame may or may not be filled with sealant. Large areas of glazing are possible using patent glazing bars, which clamp the edges of two adjacent panes and press them against the supporting framework. Aluminium, steel, wood or plastics are normally used for such glazing bars, whose capping strips are attached from outside and exert a linear contact pressure on the glass and supporting construction. An elastic sealing strip is placed between the glass and the supporting construction, and between the glass and glazing bar. This

creates a drainage system of vertical and horizontal joints that permits water to run off, unhindered, to the outside. Glazing with linear supports on two sides and the other two sides unsupported but sealed is a common arrangement. In the case of overhead glazing with a minimum fall of 2° to the horizontal, capping strips transverse to the pitch of the roof must be flattened on the upper side so that they do not hinder the water run-off. Alternatively, the capping strips across the slope can be replaced by silicone joints to ensure no obstacles. One special case of linear support is the gasket made from a permanently elastic synthetic material that forms a combination of glazing profile, patent glazing bar and sealing strip (Fig. 1e).

Glass on linear supports for overhead glazing inclined at > 10° to the vertical and for vertical glazing inclined at < 10° to the vertical is covered by the Technical Rules for the Use of Glazing on Linear Supports (TRLV). This document contains information on the design of the glazing and construction details. Provided that products listed in the Construction Products List A part 1, or those with a German national technical approval (AbZ) are used, all the TRLV requirements are satisfied and no further action to verify such glass constructions is necessary (see "Building legislation provisions", pp. 73–75). Further requirements regarding the form of construction and the configuration of the glazing enable trafficable glazing to be constructed for steps and landings provided there are linear supports on all four sides. The TRLV does not deal with facade elements fixed with adhesives to linear supports, nor glazing required to function as bracing nor curved overhead glass elements. The Technical Rules for the Design and Construction of Point-Supported Glazing (TRPV) permits the

1   Stages in the development of linear support for glass
    a Lead came
    b Putty fillet in rebate
    c Rebate with glazing bead
    d Patent glazing bar with capping strip
    e Gasket

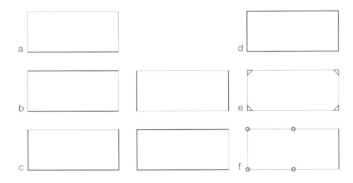

2

combination of linear support and point fixings in drilled holes.

The majority of instances of facade glazing on linear supports involves post-and-rail arrangements where the horizontal loads (wind loads) on the glazing are transferred to linear members (Figs. 3–5). The self-weight of the glazing is transferred to the supporting construction via appropriate setting blocks, i.e. point supports.

In the case of glazing on linear supports within the remit of the TRLV, the following glass products can be used:
• Float glass
• Rolled glass (wired glass, patterned glass, wired patterned glass)
• Toughened safety glass, heat-soaked toughened safety glass
• Heat-strengthened glass with national technical approval
• Laminated glass, laminated safety glass
• Multi-pane insulating glass
Monolithic glasses made from float glass, patterned glass and laminated glass may be used for vertical glazing with linear support on all sides. However, drilled holes and cutouts are only permitted in thermally toughened glasses or laminated safety glass. For safety reasons, toughened safety glass may only be used as single glazing or as the outer pane of an insulating glass unit below a height of 4 m, and then only when the area below is not normally accessible. Heat-soaked toughened safety glass must be used in all other situations.
Single glazing and the lower pane of insulating glass for overhead uses must be made from wired glass or laminated safety glass made from float glass or heat-strengthened glass to ensure adequate residual loadbearing capacity and residual stability. The minimum thickness of the PVB interlayer should be 0.76 mm.

Thinner interlayers (but not less than 0.38 mm) are only permitted in the case of support on all sides and short spans (< 0.8 m). With linear supports on two and three sides and laminated safety glass, the span may not exceed 1.2 m, otherwise linear supports on all sides and a pane aspect ratio < 3:1 is necessary. The use of wired glass is permitted in the main span direction up to a span of 0.7 m, provided a minimum edge cover of 15 mm is guaranteed at the same time. Drilled holes and cutouts are only permitted in laminated safety glass made from heat-strengthened glass and only when they are required to fix the clamping components. Deviations from the TRLV's overhead glazing requirements are possible if, for example, nets capable of intercepting and supporting larger fragments of broken glass are suspended below the glazing as protection for the circulation zone below.

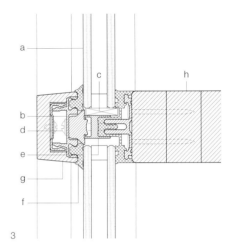

3

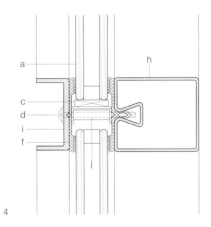

4

2   Point- and linear-type clamp fixings
    a Supported on one side
    b Supported on two sides
    c Supported on three sides
    d Supported on four sides
    e Individual clamp fixings
    f Combination of point and linear support
3   Linear clamp fixing by means of patent glazing bar with capping strip, in wood
4   Linear clamp fixing without capping strip, in steel
5   Linear clamp fixing by means of EPDM gasket
    Legend for Figs. 3–5
    a Insulating glass
    b Patent glazing bar
    c Setting block
    d Screw
    e Thermal break
    f Seal
    g Capping strip
    h Facade rail
    i Patent glazing bar
    j Spacer sleeve
    k Split gasket

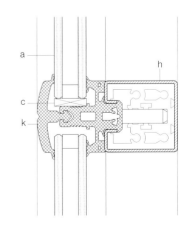

5

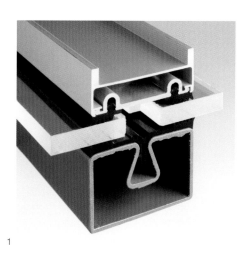

1

According to the TRLV and DIN 18516-4, glazing on linear supports must be continuously supported at least at two opposite positions. In the case of support on all sides, the edge cover must be a minimum of 10 mm, and for glazing supported on two or three sides the sum of the glass thickness plus 1/500 of the span, but at least 15 mm. All panes must be secured against slippage by means of suitable location blocks at least 5 mm thick. Vertical glazing with an unsupported bottom edge must be supported left and right. The glass footprint must be right-angled and its area must be at least equal to the edge cover multiplied by the pane thickness.

Linear-clamped glass with safety barrier function
Linear-type clamp fixings can also be used for all glazing with a safety barrier function in all the TRAV categories. Depending on the particular application, a linear-type support on one side, i.e. fixed base, or linear-type supports on two or more sides are possible.

Glass elements with linear-type clamp fixings according to the TRAV may use any construction products according to the TRLV or glass products with a national technical approval, but the thickness of the individual panes in laminated safety glass may not differ from each other by

T2: Glass configurations for linear-supported safety barrier glazing with proven impact resistance

TRAV category	Glass type	Glass configuration		Support	Glass thickness
		Impact side	Other side		
A	Insulating glass	laminated safety glass	any[1]	all sides linear	TRAV tab. 2
		TSG, LG made from TSG[2]	laminated safety glass	all sides linear	
	Single glazing	laminated safety glass		all sides linear	
B	Single glazing	laminated safety glass		fixed at base	TRAV tab. 4
C1/C2	Insulating glass	laminated safety glass, toughened safety glass	any[1]	all sides linear	TRAV tab. 2
				2 sides linear top & bottom	
	Single glazing	laminated safety glass, toughened safety glass		all sides linear	
		laminated safety glass		2 sides linear top & bottom	
				2 sides linear left & right	
C3	Insulating glass	as for category A		all sides linear	
	Single glazing				

[1] according to TRAV section 2.1;
[2] TSG, LG from TSG = toughened safety glass, laminated glass made from toughened safety glass

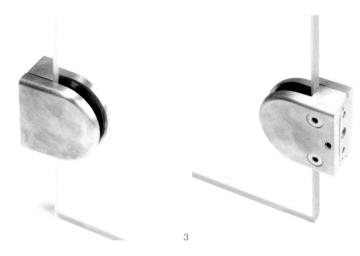

2   3

more than a factor of 1.5. The rules for heat-soaked toughened safety glass according to the TRLV also apply to glass in safety barriers. The TRAV also specifies that thermally toughened borosilicate glass with a national technical approval may be used instead of toughened safety glass made from soda-lime-silica glass.

Tab. T2 provides an overview of glass configurations with linear supports according to the TRAV for which the impact resistance has been verified. When selecting types of glass, it is essential to remember that to minimise the risk of injuries, the impact side must be made of laminated or toughened safety glass, or laminated glass made from toughened safety glass.

Details of construction glass safety barriers with linear supports are given in the TRLV. Depending on the respective category, the glass configurations for which impact resistance has been proved in tests can be found in the TRAV; however, they only apply to the constructional conditions given there (category, type of support, edge cover, etc.).

Clamped point supports
As an alternative to linear supports on all four sides, resistance to wind suction in facades can also be achieved by way of individual clamping plates. This results in two different structural systems to resist wind pressure and wind suction which must be verified separately.
Linear supports withstand the loads due to wind pressure; point supports resist the wind suction effects on the pane of glass. Edge-clamped glass infill panels in vertical glazing, the top edge of which is no more than 20 m above ground level, are dealt with in the TRPV. Moreover, the panes used may not exceed a size of 2.5 × 3.0 m. The requirements of DIN 18516-4 must also be complied with in the case

of point- and linear-type clamped pane fixings for cladding made from toughened safety glass in front of a ventilation cavity. The edge clamps resisting wind suction must be U-shaped fixings that hold all the individual panes of the glazing. The clamping area per fixing must be at least 1000 mm² for an edge cover of 25 mm.

When using individual clamp fixings only, these must be positioned along the edge of the glass or in the corners of a pane. For all loading directions perpendicular to the plane of the glass, the area of the clamp covering the glass must also be at least 1000 mm² per side and fixing for an edge cover ≥ 25 mm. Smaller clamping areas are possible, but must be verified by way of suitable tests. Clamp fixings positioned in the corners of a pane must be designed with an asymmetrical clamping area where the ratio of the sides is ≥ 1:2.5.

The glass products used may be of laminated safety glass made from toughened safety glass, heat-soaked toughened safety glass or heat-strengthened glass with a national technical approval according to the TRPV, or multi-pane insulating glass. In the latter case at least one pane must be of the aforementioned laminated safety glass. The other pane of insulating glass can also be made from the same glass or from a single pane of heat-soaked toughened safety glass. The thicknesses of the individual panes of the laminated safety glass may not deviate from each other by more than a factor of 1.5. The PVB interlayer must be at least 0.76 mm thick.

Individual clamp fixings are also used for category C1 safety barrier glazing (Figs. 2 and 3). For this situation, the TRAV specifies only laminated safety glass with drilled point fixings; such arrangements

have already been verified in tests. Monolithic toughened safety glasses with individual clamp fixings are, however, possible with a national technical approval. In the case of clamped glazing of laminated safety glass, the creep of the PVB layer can cause the clamping action to decrease over time and lead to the panes slipping out of their fixings. The panes should therefore be secured by screws or bolts in drilled holes or held in corner fixings along the bottom edge of the glass.

1   Linear support with patent glazing bar
2   Individual clamp fixing for safety barrier glass, front view
3   Individual clamp fixing for safety barrier glass, rear view

63

1

2

3

Drilled fixings

Connections with screws or bolts that carry loads by way of bearing on the side of a drilled hole are common in structural steelwork, timber construction and also in glass because they are very easy to handle on the building site. Furthermore, such connections can also be readily dismantled. The shank of the screw or bolt bears on the side of the hole to transfer the load. Glazing with point supports requires every pane to be held by at least three fixings and in the case of vertical glazing at least two fixings combined with linear support.

The requirements to be satisfied by the glass
The force transfer via bearing on the side of a hole leads to high local stresses in the glass at the point of contact between the shank of the fixing and the glass component. When using laminated safety glass, drilled holes lead to further stress concentrations in the glass. Glazing with drilled point fixings must therefore be made from toughened monolithic glass or laminated safety glass made from toughened safety

glass, heat-soaked toughened safety glass or heat-strengthened glass with a national technical approval; heat-strengthened glass is only recommended in laminated safety glass. The TRPV covers only laminated safety glasses in conjunction with the design and construction of point-supported glazing. When using monolithic toughened safety glass, it is generally best to apply the TRLV recommendations, i.e. heat-soaked toughened safety glass is recommended above a height of 4 m. The PVB interlayer must be at least 0.76 mm thick. DIN EN ISO 527-3 specifies the tear strength (> 20 N/mm^2) and the elongation at failure (> 250 %) of the interlayer. In addition, the thicknesses of the individual panes of the laminated safety glass may not differ from each other by more than a factor of 1.5. A minimum thickness of 8 mm is advisable in glass constructions with drilled holes. The offset between the drilled holes in laminated safety glass may not exceed 0.5 mm. It is subsequently necessary to work the edges. When used as overhead glazing, the lower

pane of insulating glass must be of laminated safety glass in order to ensure a certain residual loadbearing capacity. Otherwise, overhead glazing must be of laminated safety glass made from heat-strengthened glass. Tab. T3 provides an overview of the types of glass used depending on the application.

Point fixing systems
Various point fixing systems for supporting panes of glass via drilled holes are available on the market. These are distinguished according to their movability (rigid, hinged), the form of the fixing disc or the shape of the drilled hole (cylindrical, Fig. 1; cylindrical-conical, Fig. 2; cylindrical-conical with undercut, Fig. 3). Disc point fixings are made from stainless steel and have a national technical approval. The two discs in contact with the surface of the glass are joined together by a bolt or screw that passes through a cylindrical hole drilled in the glass (Fig. 1). The diameter of the disc should be at least 50 mm on both sides so that, taking

T3: Types of glass that may be used for point-supported glazing depending on the application

Application		Tough. safety glass, monolithic	Lam. safety glass made from tough. safety glass	Lam. safety glass made from heat-strength. glass
Vertical glazing without safety barrier function		×	×[1]	×[1]
Vertical glazing with safety barrier function		possible[2]	×	×
Vertical glazing made from multi-pane insulating glass without safety barrier function	inner	×	×[1]	×[1]
	outer	×	×[1]	×[1]
Vertical glazing made from multi-pane insulating glass with safety barrier function	impact side	possible[3]	×	×
	other side	×	×[1], except[4]	×[1], except[4]
Overhead glazing		–	–[5]	×[6]
Overhead glazing made from multi-pane insulating glass	top	–	–[5]	×
	bottom	×	×[1]	×[1]

[1] Not required by the building regulations
[2] Only for category C glazing
[3] Only in conjunction with laminated safety glass on the side not directly subjected to the impact
[4] Required on the impact side in the case of monolithic toughened safety glass
[5] ...except when residual loadbearing capacity is verified
[6] Use of two or more panes of glass of equal thickness ≥ 6 mm with min. 1.52 mm thick PVB interlayer

T4: Glass configurations with proven residual loadbearing capacity in the case of orthogonal support grids and the use of disc point fixings to TRPV

Disc diameter [mm]	Min. glass thickness, heat-strengthened glass [mm]	Support spacing (x-direction) [mm]	Support spacing (y-direction) [mm]
70	2 No. 6	900	750
60	2 No. 8	950	750
70	2 No. 8	1100	750
60	2 No. 10	1000	900
70	2 No. 10	1400	1000

into account the diameter of the drilled hole, an edge cover of min. 12 mm is possible. This type of fixing is covered in the TRPV. Disc fixings that cannot been verified according to the technical construction regulations specified by the building authorities (e.g. disc fixings with spherical or elastomeric joints) will require a national or European technical approval.

Drilled holes with a partly cylindrical, partly conical cross-section enable the use of countersunk point fixings that fit flush with the surface of the glass (Fig. 2). As the geometry of the hole means that the glass has a smaller footprint, higher stresses are to be expected, which must be compensated for by using thicker glass (Fig. 5c). The minimum footprint should be equal to 50 % of the glass thickness, but at least 4 mm. Installing countersunk point fixings in their drilled holes is time-consuming because they must be fitted perfectly straight, without any play. Consequently, such point fixings cannot compensate for any deformations in the pane and/or the supporting construction. Suspended overhead glazing should not be supported by countersunk point fixings because damaged panes of glass can easily slip out of the fixings, leaving no residual loadbearing capacity, no residual stability.

Cylindrical-conical holes with an undercut in toughened safety glass makes it possible to use special undercut anchors that do not pass completely through the glass (Fig. 3). Like flush point fixings, this type of fixing does not hinder the cleaning of the facade. As the hole does not pass right through the glass, there are no sealing problems at this point. This can also be achieved by disc or countersunk fixings by drilling the holes only in the inner pane of an insulating glass unit.

We distinguish between rigid or hinged supports depending on whether a point fixing can accommodate any twist in the plane of the glass. Rigid point fixings are characterised by their simple design and favourable price-performance ratio. The pane of glass can be held in place by two discs on elastic bearing pads which are then connected to the supporting construction via a threaded rod. However, this simple design leads to more assembly work on site to compensate for tolerances. The rigid fixing results in high stress concentrations around the drilled hole, especially with thin panes, but the elastic bearing pads used can reduce this to a certain extent. The fixed-end moments caused by rigid fixings must be taken into account by way of an appropriate structural model (e.g. fixed supports or stiff torsion springs) when designing the glass construction.

As an alternative, hinged point fixings can be used to reduce the restraint stresses in the pane of glass. It is essential to avoid corrosion in order to guarantee the movability of the fixing. Spherical or universal joints, or point fixings with hammerhead screws and soft rubber inlays are all possible solutions. A support with zero restraint can only be achieved with a joint whose centre of rotation is exactly in the centre of the pane, which is possible when using a rod with pinned joints at both ends. As this arrangement is difficult to implement in practice, it is essential to take into account the inherent stresses due to the offset of the centre of rotation of the joint with respect to the centre-line of the pane. Compared to rigid point fixings, hinged fixings enable tolerances in the supporting construction to be compensated for easily without introducing additional restraint stresses into the glass. The joint itself can be positioned approximately in line with the centre of the pane, directly behind the glass or further back

1 Disc point fixing in cylindrical hole
2 Countersunk point fixing in cylindrical-conical hole
3 Undercut anchor in cylindrical-conical undercut hole
4 Possible hinge positions for point fixings
  a Hinge positioned directly behind the pane with minimal eccentricity
  b Rigid support for glass
  c Hinged point fixing with large eccentricity between hinge and centre-line of glass
  d Point fixing with hinge roughly in line with the plane of the glass
5 Supporting the pane of glass
  a, c in the plane of the glass
  b, d perpendicular to plane of glass, with force transfer
  a, b on edge of glass
  c, d on face of glass

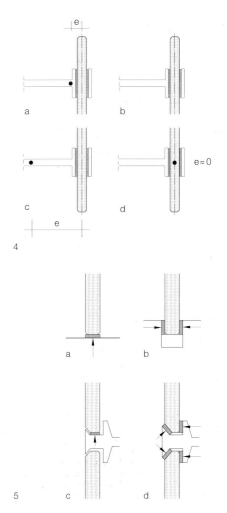

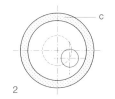
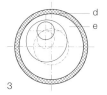
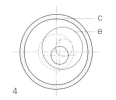

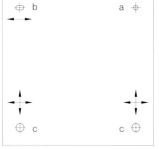

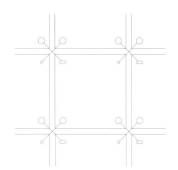

5

6

from the pane (greater eccentricity) (p. 65, Fig. 4). The eccentricity must be taken into account in the design via a corresponding moment.

Bearing
A soft, non-creep intermediate layer should always be included between the shank of the fixing and the glass in order to dissipate stress peaks around the drilled hole and transfer the bearing pressure on the side of the hole evenly to the glass. The material of this intermediate layer should be softer than glass, i.e. its modulus of elasticity must be < 70 000 N/mm^2. Prefabricated, tight-fit sleeves made from plastic or aluminium (pure aluminium, polyether ether ketone – PEEK, polyacetal – POM) can be used, or an injected material (two-part composite mortar, epoxy resin-based adhesive, glazing compound) which is mixed on site. According to the TRPV, the wall thickness of such sleeves should be min. 3 mm for disc point fixings. Such intermediate layers prevent direct contact between the glass and the steel, compensate for any irregularities in the drilled hole and guarantee that the load transfer is spread over the largest possible area. The simple installation of the prefabricated sleeves and the high level of tolerance compensation provided by materials injected on site are offset by the requirements for an accurate fit and the work involved in mixing and injection. Eccentric metal sleeves can sometimes be used to compensate for tolerances; we distinguish here between single and double eccentric sleeves. Depending on whether a single eccentric sleeve is bedded in injected material or fitted into a normal sleeve, it can be regarded as a rigid or hinged joint. As single eccentric sleeves can only compensate for tolerances to a limited extent, a so-called double eccentric sleeve – a combination of two eccentric sleeves, one

within the other and able to rotate – is used for more precise adjustment (Figs. 1–4).

A statically determinate support should always be aimed for when supporting glass by way of point fixings. Support in the plane of the glass is to be recommended here. At the top edge of the glass, a restrained fixing is combined with a partially unrestrained fixing (able to move in the horizontal direction) (Fig. 5). Any other point fixings required are designed as unrestrained fixings that enable displacement in all directions. This movement can be realised by slip layers, e.g. polytetrafluoroethylene (PTFE). Alternatively, the point fixing itself can be designed as a rod with pinned joints at both ends and anchored in the supporting construction. The force transfer between a restrained fixing and the glass can be achieved with a close-tolerance sleeve, an eccentric sleeve or by injecting a material into the gap between fixing and glass. When using multi-pane insulating glass, the compatibility with the edge seal materials must be verified. So-called spiders are frequently used in conjunction with point-supported glass facades to form a support at the intersection point of four panes (Figs. 6 and 7).

A plane is unequivocally defined geometrically by three points. Consequently, a pane of glass requires three point fixings in order to achieve statically determinate supported perpendicular to its plane. However, large-format panes in particular require four or more point fixings, which results in a statically indeterminate support condition which can therefore cause restraint stresses. Deformations of up to ±5 mm per point fixing must therefore be taken into account in addition to the planned yielding of the supports. A statically determinate support perpendicular

7

8

≤ 120°

≥ 80 mm

a

a

b

80 mm ≤ a ≤ 300 mm
100 mm ≤ b ≤ 300 mm

to the plane of the glass is very involved and only used in exceptional circumstances.

Every pane of glass held exclusively by point fixings requires at least three support points. The largest enclosed angle in the arrangement may not exceed 120° (Fig. 8). The unsupported glass edge must be at least 80 mm wide and may extend no more than 300 mm beyond the line of a triangle joining the drilled holes. The minimum distance between the drilled holes should be 80 mm. Different edge distances are required at the corner of a pane of glass: min. 80 mm in one direction, min. 100 mm in the other. DIN EN 12150-1 provides further information. According to DIN 18516-4, toughened safety glass held in place by individual clamp fixings along its edges requires fixings in drilled holes to carry the weight of the glass. The difference in the edge distances at the corners of a pane should be at least 15 mm. The edge distances of drilled holes must be at least twice the thickness of the glass and at least equal to the diameter of the drilled hole. The edge distance for undercut anchors must be at least 50 mm.

Erection
Prior to installation in a facade, all edges and drilled holes must be checked for damage. Flaws may not account for more than 10 % of the glass thickness in the case of toughened safety glass, and in the case of heat-soaked toughened safety glass, damage to the edge of the glass amounting to > 5 % of the glass thickness is not permissible. When erecting point-supported glazing with a ventilation cavity above a height of 8 m, on-site supervision of the work by a DIBt-approved inspection body is necessary. This is usually also required for facades of multi-pane insulating glass where the

outer pane is of heat-soaked toughened safety glass. All glazing must be erected free from restraint stresses. Once all the restrained and vertical fixings have been installed, all other unrestrained fixings can be mounted. All screws and bolts must be secured to prevent unintentional loosening, e.g. with Loctite. The finished facade must be checked with respect to the necessary deformation capacity and freedom from restraints.

1 Single eccentric sleeve able to rotate within metal sleeve
2 Rigidly supported single eccentric sleeve
3 Double eccentric sleeve able to rotate within plastic sleeve
4 Rigidly supported double eccentric sleeve
   Legend for Figs. 1–4
   a Metal sleeve
   b Single eccentric sleeve
   c Injected material
   d Plastic sleeve
   e Double eccentric sleeve
5 Statically determinate support in the plane of the glass by means of restrained and unrestrained supports
   a Restrained support
   b Vertical support for accommodating displacements in horizontal direction
   c Unrestrained support with allowance for displacement in both directions
6 Point-type support for glass in the facade by means of "spiders"
7 Spider: in practice a restrained support is achieved by tightening the screws accordingly – if not fully tightened the vertical support can accommodate displacements in the plane of the glass.
8 Angle and spacing definitions for glass supported by drilled point fixings

1 Undercut anchor in monolithic and laminated glass
2 Rigid disc fixing in monolithic and multi-pane insulating glass
3 Hinged countersunk fixing in monolithic and multi-pane insulating glass with the hinge in the plane of the glass
4 Disc fixing in monolithic and multi-pane insulating glass with hinge eccentric to the plane of the glass
5 Rigid countersunk fixing in monolithic and multi-pane insulating glass

Legend for Figs. 1–5:
a Monolithic or laminated safety glass
b Multi-pane insulating glass
c Clamping disc
d Screw
e Intermediate pad/seal
f Supporting construction
g Nut
h Cap
i Screw
k Countersunk head
l Edge seal
m Spherical joint
n Sealing collar
o Threaded rod
p Threaded ring
q Injected synthetic resin

6

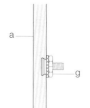

1

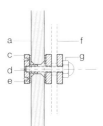

2

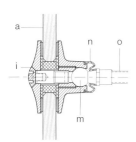

3

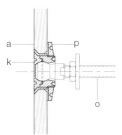

4

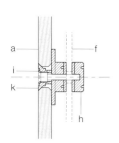

5

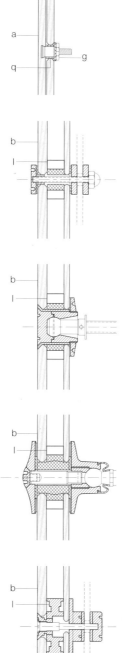

Bonded fixings

Facades fixed with adhesives exhibit improved thermal and sound insulation and better protection against driving rain. The adhesives are factory-prepared according to European Technical Approval Guideline ETAG 002, which describes the principles of the glass configurations, materials and testing methods for glass facades fixed with adhesives. In the meantime, this European guideline has been incorporated into a national standard, DIN EN 13022, but has not yet been specified as state of the art. Avoiding the on-site work means that the quality assurance demands placed on the adhesive joints can also be achieved. As a rule, facades fixed with adhesives are characterised by a higher standard of workmanship and, at the same time, lower production costs. However, as the thermal expansion coefficients of the glass and the adhesives differ, restraint stresses at the adhesive joint must always be taken into account.

Structural sealant glazing (SSG)

In Germany, glass constructions must generally satisfy high demands before they are approved. Besides proof of load-bearing capacity and serviceability, glued connections must also be checked for their durability under the given environmental conditions. Considerable experience has been gained with silicone adhesives for structural sealant glazing (SSG). SSG is a type of facade construction in which the glass is permanently connected to an adapter frame via a loadbearing, waterproof silicone joint. The glass/adhesive/frame module is attached to a post-and-rail framework. The glass can have an inorganic coating or be left uncoated. The supporting construction consists of anodised or powder-coated aluminium or stainless steel sections.

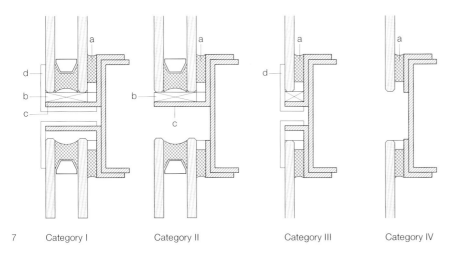

7   Category I   Category II   Category III   Category IV

The black silicones used are made from a polymer base plus chalk, silicic acid and soot fillers and further substances. The fillers stabilise the polymer so that a strength of about 1 N/mm^2 can be guaranteed; they also ensure a workable viscosity. The black colour of the silicone is due to the addition of soot; the butterfly test can be used to assess the quality of the mix of two-part silicone products. This test involves pouring some of the silicone mix onto a sheet of white paper which is then folded, flattened and then unfolded. A uniform black colour indicates complete mixing of the components. Production is simple and cost-effective. Transparent silicones are possible in principle, but require more expensive polymers (resins); this is why they have not become established for facades. Tab. T5 (p. 70) shows the main properties of the silicones, the requirements adhesive joints have to satisfy and how the less favourable properties of the adhesives are dealt with in practice.

Owing to their adhesive properties, coatings on glass can no longer be classed as pure glass surfaces. A thorough adhesion test is carried out to prove whether they are suitable for long-term use. In destructive testing of aged and non-aged small-format specimens, cohesive failure within the adhesive layer is proof of its good adhesion to the respective surface. In the case of low E coatings, the coating must be removed from the edges to enable silicone joints in SSG facades. Glasses from which the coating has been removed are suitable for gluing and the service lives of such glued joints are not affected.

Building legislation and tests
The European Technical Approval Guideline for bonded glass constructions, ETAG 002, distinguishes between four categories of glued glass constructions depending on the way in which the loads are carried (Figs. 6 and 7).

Approval for categories I and II is possible in Germany. In these categories, the silicone joints do not carry the weight of the glazing, only transfer the wind loads to the supporting construction. Categories III and IV are characterised by the fact that the loadbearing silicone joint carries both the weight of the glazing and the wind loads. Only single glazing is used here. In addition, mechanical retention of the panes of glass is necessary above a height of 8 m – to prevent complete glass elements from falling. This is achieved with peripheral strips, additional point fixings, hooks in ground recesses or undercut anchors. Figs. 2–4 (p. 70) show silicone joints with and without additional mechanical retention. The omission of this is customary and permitted in many European countries. Various SSG systems and also some individual silicone products are approved at national or European level (AbZ, ETA). Deviating systems and adhesives can be awarded individual approvals by the respective federal state building authority. Deviations from the systems approved by the building authorities can be found in the surface qualities of the jointing

6   Mechanical support for carrying the weight of the
    glass in a category II SSG facade
7   Bonded facade categories to ETAG 002:
    I and II: weight of glass carried via mechanical
    support
    III and IV: weight of glass carried by adhesive
    I and III: additional mechanical retention
    II and IV: no mechanical retention
    a   Adhesive
    b   Setting block
    c   Mechanical support for weight of glass
    d   Mechanical retainer

1

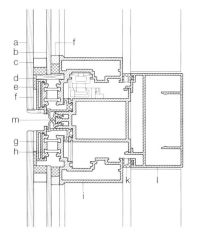

2

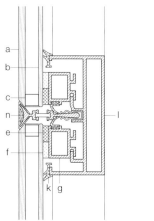

3

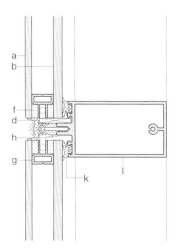

4

components, special joint geometries and loads on the joints other than just wind loads.

During the planning phase, the adhesive manufacturer first checks the materials to be bonded and the proposed dimensions of the adhesive joints. Based on this information, he can then recommend a suitable silicone product. In addition, tests on small-format samples are necessary to check the product quality (hardness, density, shrinkage, etc.), the strength of non-aged samples, the residual strength after ageing (e.g. UV radiation, moisture, cleaning agents) and compatibility with the adjoining materials (e.g. PVB interlayer). One of the characteristics that has to be verified is the minimum strength of the adhesive joint according to ETAG 002 – on no account is an adhesion failure permitted in a destructive test of a sample; to confirm adequate adhesion to the respective surfaces, only a cohesive failure within the adhesive substance is permitted. Based on this, recommendations regarding cleaning and surface treatments can be made. Quality assurance is supplemented by tests during the preparation of the silicones.

Outlook
Other adhesive systems such as epoxy resins, polyurethanes or acrylates may represent alternatives to the customary silicones in applications where a different strength or colour is required. The transfer of glued joint geometries from other sectors (e.g. automotive industry, aircraft construction, railway rolling stock) to glass in construction, the exploitation of the advantages of adhesive technologies and studies into the adhesive properties and durability of other materials in conjunction with glass could lead to new types of structures and a wealth of options in the medium-term. Adhesive joints with transparent adhesives permit completely invisible glass-to-glass connections. One good example of this is the memorial to the victims of the Madrid terrorist attacks of 11 March 2004 (Fig. 5). This structure, approximately elliptical on plan and 11 m high, is built with glass blocks glued together with a transparent UV-curing acrylate. The bonding of glass to other materials may also leave the original surfaces visible (Fig. 1). Composite glass-and-plastic elements (panes of glass either side of a polycarbonate

T5: Properties of SSG silicones in relation to load-carrying adhesives for facades

Requirement	Properties of silicone	Construction
	Creep	Mechanical support
Resistance to chemical media	Good resistance	
	Low strength with respect to tension and combined tension and shear stresses	Sufficiently large adhesive faces
Accommodation of component tolerances		Minimum joint width
Weather resistance	Permanently weather-resistant	
Component deformations	Elastic over the range -40 to +150°C	
	Damaged by permanent moisture	Open joints to allow drying out
Thermal stability	Resistant up to 200°C	
UV resistance	UV-resistant	

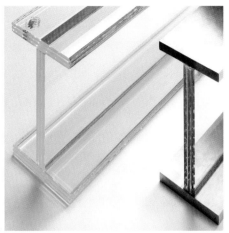

core), the surfaces of which are glued together with a special transparent polyurethane, can satisfy anti-bandit requirements. In comparison to conventional security glasses, such composite arrangements result in lighter and more slender cross-sections offering the same or even better functionality. Constructions whose loadbearing capacity relies on the interaction of different materials are known as hybrid structural systems. These constructions are immensely important for the building industry. The combination of different materials within one loadbearing system or component give rise to new, worthwhile properties.

Linear components (glass fins, glass beams) are mainly produced in the form of multi-ply laminated glasses with a rectangular cross-section. The low redundancy in such a loadbearing construction and the less-than-optimum cross-sectional form of such components have led to the development of new, alternative loadbearing members. A significant improvement in the loadbearing behaviour can be achieved by bonding different materials together to create a non-rectangular cross-section.

Planar glass-plastic composites can be connected to create various cross-sections. The inner ply is of transparent plastic, the two outer plies are of glass. Suitable adhesives are available for connecting plastics and glass. This results in load-carrying transparent components that combine the strength and durability of glass with the ductile properties of the plastic, and hence guarantee a margin of safety at the point of failure. Advanced warning of the failure of building components – through the appearance of cracks – is desirable for buildings, as is a residual loadbearing capacity even if the glass is completely broken.

Bonded joints in hybrid components of glass and steel are also being investigated. Resembling a rolled steel section, they have a web of glass that is bonded over its full length to steel flanges. A suitable jointing method bonds the glass into the component as a load-carrying element. Basically, the cross-sectional form and the dimensions can be adapted to suit the particular circumstances of the application. The planned forms have a higher geometrical stiffness and the necessary redundancy owing to the optimum combination of materials (Fig. 6). Alternative, glued composite sections thus result in a better load-carrying capacity compared to conventional, rectangular glass beams.

1   Invisible bonds by way of UV- and light-curing acrylates between glass and metals with different surface finishes (left to right: polished chromium-plated brass, turned stainless steel, anodised aluminium)
2   Vertical section through an SSG facade without additional mechanical retention
3   Vertical section through an SSG facade with additional mechanical retention and sealing by way of a gasket
4   Vertical section through an SSG facade with additional mechanical retention to the inner pane of an insulating glass unit and joint sealed with sealing compound; it is not necessary to bond the inner pane here.
    Legend for Figs. 2–4
    a   Outer pane
    b   Inner pane
    c   Edge seal to insulating glass
    d   Setting block
    e   Backing strip
    f   Silicone joint
    g   Steel or aluminium element
    h   Thermal break
    i   Modular frame
    k   Seal
    l   Rail
    m   Seal
    n   Gasket providing mechanical retention and sealing function
5   Facade with transparent sealing/bonding compound; glass memorial for the victims of the terrorist attacks of 11 March 2004, Madrid (E), 2007, Estudio FAM, Schlaich Bergermann & Partner
6   Bonded all-glass and glass/metal I-sections

Building legislation provisions

The use of glass as a construction and loadbearing element is a relatively new form of construction. In contrast to established building materials, e.g. reinforced concrete, there are no comprehensive regulations. The critical aspect for architects and engineers is to know whether the chosen glass product or application is covered or not covered by the technical rules and regulations. Depending on the building project, this could have a considerable influence on the planning phase – in terms of both time and budget. Knowledge of the status of the regulations is essential in every situation. However, project teams should not allow themselves to be put off: applications not covered by the technical regulations are not prohibited, but simply call for a somewhat different approach.

An overview of German legislation

In Germany, building legislation is in the hands of the individual federal states. Each state's building regulations (LBO) are based on the Model Building Code (MBO) agreed on by the ministers responsible for building and contain essentially the same provisions. The MBO calls for buildings and structures to be designed, erected, modified and maintained in such a way that public safety and order, in particular life, health and the natural resources essential to life, are not endangered (Model Building Code – MBO

– Nov 2002 edition; all the extracts given below are taken from this edition). All building products and forms of construction used must comply with this principle.

The Construction Products List (BRL) is the instrument with which the technical rules for building products and forms of construction are publicised by the German Institute of Building Technology (DIBt) in agreement with the supreme federal state building authorities. There are three lists, A, B and C, and they are republished every year.

The List of Technical Construction Regulations (LTB) supplements the building products specified in the BRLs; it contains the technical rules for planning, designing and constructing buildings and structures and their components. Although each federal state has its own LTB, based on a Model List of Technical Construction Regulations (MLTB), they essentially conform with each other. But as the time of implementation varies and provisions may be added or removed, it is advisable to inquire about the legislation concerning the use of glass as a construction material in the respective federal state. The current edition of the MLTB contains a total of five application standards and regulations that affect the use of glass in building (Tab. T1).

T1: Current application standards and regulations according to the MLTB, Feb 2008 edition

Title	Edition
DIN 18516-4: Back-ventilated, non-loadbearing, external enclosures of buildings, made from tempered safety glass panels; requirements and testing	February 1990
Technical Rules for the Use of Glazing on Linear Supports (TRLV)	August 2006
Technical Rules for Glass in Safety Barriers (TRAV)	January 2003
Technical Rules for the Design and Construction of Point-Supported Glazing (TRPV)	August 2006
DIN V 11535-1: Greenhouses – Part 1: Basic principles for design and construction	February 1998

T2: Classification of building products according to the Model Building Code (MBO)

Regulated	National				Other	European
	Non-regulated					According to harmonised European standards or with ETA[4]
	General	No significant requirements or acknowledged test methods	Of minor importance for building legislation			
Construction Products List A part 1	–	Construction Products List A part 2	List C		Acknowledged codes of practice	Construction Products List B
Technical rules	ZiE[1] or AbZ[2]	AbP[3]	No verification of applicability		No verification of applicability	Technical rules and restricted applicability
	Attestation of conformity Ü-mark			No attestation of conformity No Ü-mark		Proof of conformity CE marking

[1] ZiE: Individual approval
[2] AbZ: National technical approval
[3] AbP: National test certificate
[4] ETA: European Technical Approval

Building products of glass

According to the MBO, the term "building products" describes "building materials, building components and constructions that are produced for permanent use in buildings and structures". Furthermore, this term encompasses "prefabricated constructions made from building materials and building components which are produced in order to be connected to the ground such as prefabricated houses, prefabricated garages and silos". Prefabricated safety barrier glazing, i.e. factory-assembled systems consisting of the supporting structure for the glass and the glazing, falls into this category.

The MBO divides building products into three categories:
• Category 1: Building products that do not deviate, or only insignificantly, from the technical rules, which are labelled with the Ü-mark (Fig. 1). Such products are specified in BRL A part 1 (Tab. T3).
• Category 2: Building products that may be marketed and traded according to European regulations are specified in BRL B and are labelled with the CE marking (Fig. 2) as proof of their con-

formity. However, these building products require application standards or regulations because otherwise they would be regarded as non-regulated forms of construction. One example is heat-strengthened glass (Tabs. T4 and T5).
• Category 3: Other building products that play only a subsidiary role in terms of technical safety provisions, do not require verification of applicability and may not be labelled with the Ü-mark. The acknowledged codes of practice cover these products but they are not specified in BRL A.
Building products that cannot be assigned to any of these three categories are classed as non-regulated. Owing to the changeover from national to harmonised European standards for the use of glass in building, it is possible to encounter two different terms for one and the same basic glass product made from soda-lime-silica glass. For instance, what was in the past referred to as plate glass in the national DIN standard now corresponds to float glass according to DIN EN 572. Patterned glass, patterned wired glass and polished wired glass were in the past referred to in

the national DIN standard as cast glass. The glass products listed in Tab. T4 represent the majority of glass building products used for glass constructions. However, there are some restrictions placed on the use of glass. Not every building product is approved for every application. Where this is the case, such products are treated as non-regulated building products. There are, of course, further glass products that do not appear in this table because they are used only rarely for applications in the building industry (e.g. fusing glass). Please consult the manufacturer regarding the standards or regulations that apply in such cases.

1   German Ü-mark
2   CE marking

T3: Extract from Construction Products List A part 1, edition 2008/1 (regulated building products)

No.	Building product	Technical rules	Attestation of conformity	Verification of applicability in the case of significant deviation from the technical rules
1	2	3	4	5
11.10	Basic products made from soda-lime-silica glass to EN 572-9[1] • Float glass • Polished wired glass • Drawn sheet glass • Patterned glass • Wired patterned glass • Profiled glass	Annex 11.5	ÜH	Z

[1] For use according to the Technical Rules for the Use of Glazing on Linear Supports (TRLV), the Technical Rules for Glass in Safety Barriers (TRAV) and for greenhouses according to DIN V 11535-1
ÜH: Manufacturer's declaration of conformity
Z: National technical approval

Author's remark: Building products made from glass are listed in chapter 11 of Construction Products List A part 1. The consecutive number 11.10 describes basic products made from soda-lime-silica glass to EN 572-9. Columns 3 to 5 specify additional application conditions, the nature of the attestation of conformity and the verification of applicability in the case of significant deviation from the technical rules.

T4: Status of regulations covering building products made from glass

Building product	Status of regulations	Explanations
Float glass	regulated by DIN EN 572-1/2/8/9	Clear and tinted float glass made from soda-lime-silica glass.
Polished wired glass	regulated by DIN EN 572-1/3/8/9	Clear polished wired glass made from soda-lime-silica glass.
Patterned glass	regulated by DIN EN 572-1/5/8/9	Clear and tinted patterned glass made from soda-lime-silica glass.
Patterned wired glass	regulated by DIN EN 572-1/6/8/9	With textured or smooth-rolled surface (wired glass), clear or tinted, made from soda-lime-silica glass.
Drawn sheet glass	regulated by DIN EN 572-1/4/8/9	Also includes "new antique" sheet glass plus drawn sheet glass for renovation work (sheet glass with the flaws so typical of historical production), clear or tinted, made from soda-lime-silica glass.
Profiled glass	regulated by DIN EN 572-1/7/9	Clear and tinted profiled glass made from soda-lime-silica glass, textured surface and wire inlay possible.
Toughened safety glass and heat-soaked toughened safety glass	regulated by DIN EN 12150	Thermally toughened soda-lime-silica safety glass made from the following glass products: float glass, drawn sheet glass and patterned glass plus coated glass to DIN EN 1096-1 and enamelled glass.
Heat-strengthened glass	Building product with CE marking according to harmonised standard DIN EN 1863; limited regulation according to Technical Construction Regulations	Can be used as a regulated building product within the scope of the Technical Construction Regulations under the following conditions: • When assuming the tensile bending stress currently permitted for float glass in the design. • When used as multi-pane insulating glass with linear supports on all sides with an area of max. 1.6 m^2 or as laminated safety glass with an area of max. 1.0 m^2 Other uses of heat-strengthened glass are possible when the product has been awarded a national technical approval for the respective application.
Chemically toughened glass	Building product with CE marking according to harmonised standard DIN EN 12337; non-regulated according to Technical Construction Regulations	Usage according to the Technical Construction Regulations is possible when the building product has been awarded a national technical approval for the respective application.
Laminated safety glass	regulated by DIN EN 14449	PVB interlayer with tear strength > 20 N/mm^2 and elongation at failure > 250 %; coloured interlayers possible; made from the following glass products: basic glass products made from soda-lime-silica glass to DIN EN 572 (except for profiled glass) plus toughened and heat-soaked toughened safety glass. Coated and enamelled glass: the treated surface should not be in contact with the PVB interlayer.
Laminated glass	regulated by DIN EN 14449	Made from the following glass products: basic glass products made from soda-lime-silica glass to DIN EN 572 (except for profiled glass) plus toughened, heat-soaked toughened and laminated safety glasses, also coated glass.
Multi-pane insulating glass	regulated by DIN EN 1279	Made from the following glass products: basic glass products made from soda-lime-silica glass to DIN EN 572 (except for profiled glass) plus toughened, heat-soaked toughened and laminated safety glasses, also laminated and coated glass; fittings in the cavity and gas fillings are possible.
Borosilicate glass	Building product with CE marking according to harmonised standard DIN EN 1748-1; non-regulated according to Technical Construction Regulations	Can be used according to the Technical Construction Regulations when the product has been awarded a national technical approval for the respective application; float, drawn, rolled or cast variations are possible, clear or tinted.
Alkaline earth glass	Building product with CE marking according to harmonised standard DIN EN 14178; non-regulated according to Technical Construction Regulations	Can be used according to the Technical Construction Regulations when the product has been awarded a national technical approval for the respective application; produced in the form of clear or tinted float glass.
Toughened safety glass made from borosilicate glass or alkaline earth glass	Building product with CE marking according to harmonised standards DIN EN 13024 and DIN EN 14321; non-regulated according to Technical Construction Regulations	Can be used according to the Technical Construction Regulations when the product has been awarded a national technical approval for the respective application; coated or enamelled glass may be used.
Glass ceramics	Building product with CE marking according to harmonised standard DIN EN 1748-2; non-regulated according to Technical Construction Regulations	Can be used according to the Technical Construction Regulations when the product has been awarded a national technical approval for the respective application; float, drawn, rolled or cast variations are possible, transparent or translucent, clear or tinted.
Coated glass	regulated by DIN EN 1096	Glasses with thin, permanent coatings made from inorganic materials; e.g. low E glass, glass with anti-reflection coating, self-cleaning glass, dichroic glass; does not include enamelling; further processing is possible to form toughened, heat-soaked toughened and laminated safety glass, laminated glass and multi-pane insulating glass.
Enamelled glass	Only regulated glasses may be used	Enamelling (silk-screen printing) over all or part of the surface is possible; the permissible tensile bending strength of the glass must be reduced for the enamelled side in the design.
Obscured glass	Only regulated glasses may be used; contact with building authority responsible is recommended	Obscuring by way of etching or sand-blasting (the latter in particular represents an intervention in the glass surface); any stipulations must be clarified with the building authority responsible.
Bent glass	non-regulated	Usage requires individual approval apart from the few exceptions; bent glass should not exhibit any inherent stresses after the bending process and, if applicable, lamination.
Glass blocks, thick pressed glass	regulated by DIN 18175 and DIN 4243	A new document for both building products is already available (DIN EN 1051 parts 1 and 2), but has not yet been introduced into building regulations.
Prefabricated safety barrier glazing	regulated by TRAV, with the exception of sections 6.2 and 6.3.2 b and c	Prefabricated safety barrier glazing according to the TRAV whose resistance to impact-like actions has already been proved or can be proved by calculation.

Forms of construction with glass

Forms of construction, which are defined in the MBO as "the assembly of building products to form buildings or structures or parts thereof", are categorised as being either regulated and non-regulated.

The Technical Construction Regulations describe the regulated forms of construction and specify their framework conditions. At the moment, however, the status of the regulation of glass constructions is unsatisfactory because the sets of rules that have been introduced cover only a fraction of the possibilities for using glass in building (Tab. T1). In order to expand the restricted range of applications, a new series of standards has been in preparation since 2003: DIN 18008 "Glass in building" will eventually be published in seven parts and will also cover those glass constructions that today are classed as non-regulated and therefore require additional verification of applicability. However, the date on which this series of standards will come into force has not yet been fixed.

Tab. T6 lists forms of glass construction together with their regulatory documents, and explains the important conditions that apply to each form. But restrictions – in some cases considerable – apply even to the regulated forms of construction. An assembly that deviates significantly from the stipulations of the Technical Construc-tion Regulations is classed as a non-regulated form of construction. Details of the implementation as a regulated form of construction can be found in the respective regulations.

The Technical Rules for the Use of Glazing on Linear Supports (TRLV) applies to glazing – both vertical and overhead – that is supported continuously on at least two opposite sides (Tab. T6). However, the provisions of the TRLV do not have to be applied to vertical glazing whose top edge is no more than 4 m above a circulation zone, although the stability of such glazing must still be verified according to the state of the art. And such vertical glazing adjacent to public circulation areas, e.g. places of work, places of assembly, nurseries, schools, must always be made from toughened or laminated safety glass.

Overhead glazing that could be subjected to the loads of persons performing cleaning, maintenance or repair work (glazing for occasional foot traffic) must also be checked for such loads and is not fully covered by the TRLV. Suitability must be verified by way of tests and is usually based on the principles for testing and certifying components for constant or occasional foot traffic (GS-BAU-18). As this verification is carried out within the scope of an individual approval (ZiE, see p. 80), the supreme building authority can, however, also demand tests that deviate from GS-BAU-18. Bavaria is an exception: in this state trafficable glazing is classed as a regulated form of construction when it complies with the TRLV and DIN 4426 and tests according to GS-BAU-18 have established compliance.

Glazing that is designed to be walked upon constantly and forms part of a circulation zone of course carries imposed loads that are much higher than those on glazing where, for example, only occasional maintenance or cleaning is necessary. Such glazing is covered by the TRLV to a limited extent only and again requires verification of applicability once the glass falls outside the scope of the regulations (Fig. 1).

Vertical glazing that also has to function as a safety barrier is covered by the Technical Rules for Glass in Safety Barriers (TRAV). These rules require proof that the glass can resist impact-type actions as well. In principle, testing is not necessary when one of the two variations given in the rules applies:
Firstly, the TRAV contains tables of glazing forms whose impact resistance has been proved in tests, and such glazing can be used in safety barrier constructions without the need for any further verification. Secondly, there is the option of verification by means of stress tables, which can also be found in the TRAV. However, this is

1   Example of an all-glass bridge which because of its construction and component dimensions lies outside the scope of the trafficable glazing provisions of the TRLV; Schwabisch Hall (D), 2004, Kraft + Kraft Architekten

T5: Extract from Construction Products List B part 1, edition 2008/1 (building products within the scope of harmonised standards according to the European Construction Products Directive)

No.	Building product		Steps and classes neces-sary depending on type of use
	Designation	Standard	
1	2	3	4
1.11.5	Heat-strengthened soda-lime-silica glass	EN 1863-2 (Oct 2004), implemented in Germany in the form of DIN EN 1863-2 (Jan 2005)	Annex 01[1]

[1] Annex 01 makes reference to the federal state building regulations with respect to the conditions of use.

T6: Status of regulations covering forms of glass construction

Form of construction	Status of regulations	Explanations
Linear-supported vertical glazing	regulated by TRLV	Glued, linear-supported vertical glazing and glazing designed to act as bracing are non-regulated. Single glazing made from basic soda-lime-silica glass products or laminated glass must have linear support on all sides. Heat-soaked toughened safety glass must be used instead of monolithic toughened safety glass above an installation height of 4 m. This also applies to the external pane of multi-pane insulating glass. Additional requirements apply in the case of vertical glazing with a safety barrier function.
Linear-supported overhead glazing	regulated by TRLV	Glued, linear-supported overhead glazing, curved overhead glazing and glazing designed to act as bracing are non-regulated. Single glazing must be made from wired glass (main span max. 0.7 m) or laminated safety glass made from float or heat-strengthened glass according to a national technical approval. The laminated safety glass may have linear support on two sides up to a span of 1.2 m; linear support on all sides is necessary for longer spans; but the pane aspect ratio may not exceed 3:1. Deviations from the application conditions without additional verification of applicability are possible when suitable measures are taken (e.g. safety nets) to prevent larger fragments of glass falling onto circulation areas. Additional requirements apply in the case of glazing for constant or occasional foot traffic.
Linear-supported glazing for constant foot traffic	regulated by TRLV	Only glass steps or landing elements with continuous linear support on all sides are regulated. The dimensions are limited to a maximum length of 1.5 m and a maximum width of 0.4 m. In the case of deviations from the rectangular form, these dimensions apply to a rectangle enclosing the glazing. Only laminated safety glass with at least three laminations may be used; the topmost pane (made from toughened safety or heat-strengthened glass) in this configuration must be min. 10 mm thick, the two panes underneath min. 12 mm thick. The glazing may not be subjected to vehicular traffic nor heavy permanent loads nor an increased risk of impacts.
Linear-supported glazing for occasional foot traffic	non-regulated (except in Bavaria: proof according to TRLV and DIN 4426)	Overhead glazing that is not subjected to constant foot traffic, but instead only persons performing cleaning, maintenance or repair work. Toughened or laminated safety glass should be used for the panes of a multi-pane insulating glass unit, single glazing must be made from laminated safety glass made from float or heat-strengthened glass according to a national technical approval. An individual approval is required for such glazing.
Linear-supported vertical glazing with safety barrier function	regulated by TRAV	Linear-supported vertical glazing in the meaning of the TRLV which is additionally secured to prevent a sideways fall. The glass products that may be used are given in sections 6.3 and 6.4 of the TRAV.
Loadbearing glass balustrades with continuous handrail and safety barrier function	regulated by TRAV	Glass balustrades that are supported at their base by a linear clamp fixing; the individual panes of glass must be of laminated safety glass and interconnected by means of a continuous handrail enclosing the top edge.
Balustrade infill panels of glass with safety barrier function	regulated by TRAV	The balustrade infill panels must have linear and/or point supports on at least two opposite sides. Laminated safety glass, multi-pane insulating glass or toughened safety glass (only in the case of support on all sides) may be used depending on the application.
Point-supported vertical and overhead glazing	regulated by TRPV	Only glazing with maximum dimensions of 2.5 x 3.0 m and its top edge no more than 20 m above ground level is regulated. Laminated safety glass made from toughened safety and heat-soaked toughened safety glass plus heat-strengthened glass according to a national technical approval and multi-pane insulating glass for applications with clamped edge fixings are the glass products that may be used. Each pane must be supported by at least three point fixings and may not provide any bracing function. Additional requirements apply in the case of vertical glazing with a safety barrier function and glazing for constant or occasional foot traffic.
Point-supported vertical glazing with safety barrier function	non-regulated	Exception: point-supported balustrade infill panels for internal applications are regulated according to the TRAV. Other forms of construction require a national technical approval or an individual approval.
Point-supported glazing for constant foot traffic	non-regulated	National technical approval or individual approval required.
Point-supported glazing for occasional foot traffic	non-regulated	National technical approval or individual approval required.
Cladding made from heat-soaked toughened safety glass fitted in front of ventilation cavity	regulated by DIN 18516-4	Linear- or point-type fixings (without drilled holes) are possible. The full thickness of each pane of glass must be enclosed or held by the fixing.
Glued glass constructions	non-regulated	European Technical Approval (ETA), national technical approval or individual approval required.
Loadbearing elements made from glass, e.g. beams, columns, fins, shear diaphragms	non-regulated	Individual approval required.

TRLV: Technical Rules for the Use of Glazing on Linear Supports
TRAV: Technical Rules for Glass in Safety Barriers
TRPV: Technical Rules for the Design and Construction of Point-Supported Glazing

1

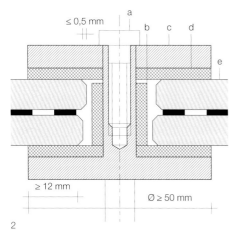

2

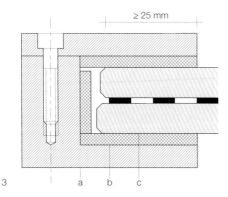

3

restricted to certain glass dimensions and thicknesses with precisely defined support conditions. The impact resistance of many safety barrier constructions therefore has to be assured by way of testing, the costs of which and the time required must be taken into account in the planning process (see pp. 80–81).

The Technical Rules for the Design and Construction of Point-Supported Glazing (TRPV) apply to vertical and overhead glazing in which all the panes of glass are supported exclusively by means of individual mechanical fixings. Such fixings can take the form of discs on both sides of the glass connected via a bolt or screw passing through a cylindrical hole drilled in the glass, or small U-shaped clamps that grip the edge of the glass (Figs. 2 and 3). Point-supported glazing with a safety barrier function or designed for constant or occasional foot traffic plus other types of point fixings are not mentioned in the TRPV.
DIN 18516-4 "Back-ventilated, non-load-bearing, external enclosures of buildings, made from tempered safety glass panels; requirements and testing" covers cladding produced from heat-soaked toughened safety glass. This standard enables

the use of clamped supports – linear- and point-type – on two, three and four sides, without drilling holes in the glass (Fig. 1). However, precisely defined design rules must be complied with. It is also important for the user to know that the erection of point-supported cladding made from heat-soaked toughened safety glass in front of a ventilation cavity must be supervised by an approved body at heights exceeding 8 m above ground level.

Non-regulated building products and forms of construction

Building products made from glass that are not listed in BRL A part 1, and are hence classed as non-regulated building products, are not necessarily excluded from use in glass constructions. The same applies to non-regulated forms of construction. Approval instruments have been developed for these cases, which despite the absence of regulations enable their use in practical building applications and hence pave the way for innovative and special forms of construction.

The so-called verification of applicability for building products or forms of construction can be effected by one of the following:

---

1 Point-supported toughened safety glass cladding in front of ventilation cavity according to DIN 18516-4, Jewish Community & Arts Centre, Würzburg (D), 2006, Grellmann Kriebel Teichmann Architekten
2 Sketch of the principle of a disc fixing according to the TRPV
  a Screw
  b Sleeve ($d_{wall} \geq 3$ mm)
  c Clamping disc
  d Elastic bearing pad (e.g. EPDM)
  e Lam. safety glass with min. 0.76 mm PVB interlayer
3 Sketch of the principle of an edge clamp fixing according to the TRPV
  a Edge clamp fixing
  b Elastic bearing pad (e.g. EPDM)
  c Lam. safety glass with min. 0.76 mm PVB interlayer

T7: Extract from Construction Products List A part 2, edition 2008/1 (non-regulated building products that can be assessed according to acknowledged testing methods)

No.	Building product	Verification of applicability	Acknowledged testing method according to…	Attestation of conformity
1	2	3	4	5
2.43	Prefabricated safety barrier glazing according to the TRAV whose resistance to impact-like actions is to be proven by testing	P	Technical Rules for Glass in Safety Barriers (TRAV), edition 2003/01, sections 6.2 and 6.3.2 b and c	ÜH

P: National test certificate
ÜH: Manufacturer's declaration of conformity

Author's remark: Prefabricated safety barrier glazing is a factory-assembled glass support construction including glazing and is regarded as a building product.

4   Trafficable glazing with national technical approval
     (SGG Lite Floor)
5   Structural sealant glazing facade, Hamilton House
     in the Broadgate district of London (GB), 2004,
     Skidmore, Owings & Merrill

- National test certificate (AbP)
- National technical approval (AbZ)
- Individual approval (ZiE)
- European Technical Approval (ETA) –
  an additional instrument at European
  level

Only the non-regulated building products
specified in BRL C do not require verification of applicability nor attestation of conformity. Such products play only a minor
role in satisfying the requirements of the
building regulations and may not be
labelled with a Ü-mark.

National test certificate (AbP)

A national test certificate can be issued
for building products or forms of construction that can be assessed according to
acknowledged methods of testing and
whose use does not have to satisfy significant requirements regarding the safety
of buildings or structures. They are specified in parts 2 (building products) and 3
(forms of construction) of BRL A (Tab.
T7). There are no Technical Construction
Regulations or acknowledged codes of
practice for these products or constructions. Certificates are issued by testing
institutes approved by the building
authorities and are generally valid for
five years. One example that falls into

this category is glass safety barriers,
which require experimental proof of
impact resistance but do not deviate significantly from the constructional stipulations of the TRAV.

National technical approval (AbZ)

The German Institute of Building Technology (DIBt) is responsible for issuing these
approvals. A national technical approval
is required for building products and
forms of construction for which there are
no acknowledged codes of practice or
where the products or constructions deviate significantly from accepted standards
and a national test certificate is not possible. Many everyday glass products, e.g.
heat-strengthened glass, laminated safety
glass made from heat-strengthened glass,
or laminated safety glass with special
interlayers whose properties deviate from
a PVB interlayer, have a national technical approval, also non-regulated forms of
construction with identical designs. Typical examples are canopy systems in different variations, point-supported glazing
where certain stipulations regarding
dimensions and support conditions have
to be adhered to, or trafficable glazing
(Fig. 4). Obtaining a national technical
approval is a relatively costly and time-

consuming business and is therefore only
advisable for a certain form of construction when it is to be used repeatedly in
the same way. The approval applies only
to the system of the applicant and not to
identical copies by other manufacturers.
It describes the object of the approval
with its components and area of application, and stipulates dimensions, design
and construction. Approvals for both
building products and forms of construction are generally valid for five years.

European Technical Approval (ETA)

In addition to technical approval at
national level, there is also an alternative
at European level, the European Technical Approval (ETA). Guidelines are available for some building products or forms
of construction (European Technical
Approval Guideline, ETAG), and these
simplify the approval procedure. Structural sealant glazing (SSG, Fig. 5) is
among the forms of glass construction for
which an ETAG has been drawn up. EU
member states issued their first national
approvals in the late 1980s. For some
time now there has been the option of
obtaining an ETA via the approval guideline
for glued forms of glass construction
(ETAG 002). In Germany, as is the case

T8: National verification of usability

	National test certificate according to Model Building Code (MBO) cl. 19	National technical approval according to Model Building Code (MBO) cl. 18	Individual approval according to Model Building Code (MBO) cl. 20
Authority responsible	Testing institute approved by the building authority according to MBO cl. 25	German Institute of Building Technology (DIBt)	Supreme building authority
Object of application	Non-regulated building products and forms of construction that are not required to satisfy significant safety requirements or can be assessed according to acknowl- edged methods of testing.	Non-regulated building products and forms of construction	Non-regulated building products and forms of construction
Period of validity	Normally 5 years	Normally 5 years	Once only for building product/form of construction described in application

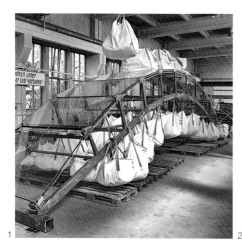

with national technical approvals, the DIBt is also responsible for ETAs. ETAG 002 specifies the requirements that glued glass constructions have to fulfil. The applicant must prove to the DIBt that these criteria are complied with. The guideline covers only adhesive joints in which the glass, which may be coated, is factory-bonded to a metal supporting frame by means of a two-part silicone adhesive. The ensuing facade element is then attached to a traditional post-and-rail construction, the structure of which is at best hardly visible from outside. In contrast to a national technical approval, the content of the ETA is, however, restricted to the specification of the product. Stipulations regarding usage and dimensions are not included and are the responsibility of the respective EU member state in which the project is being realised. In the German application rules there are restrictions on certain forms of construction and also with respect to the installation height. In addition, the silicone adhesive used itself requires a national technical approval if it is to be used in this form of construction. An ETA is generally valid for a period of five years throughout the European Union and the countries of the European Economic Area (EEA). However, glued glass constructions can continue to be built based on the stipulations of a national test certificate or individual approval.

Individual approval (ZiE)
When a national technical approval, European Technical Approval or national test certificate is not available for non-regulated building products or forms of construction, or those that deviate significantly from the Technical Construction Regulations, their use or application requires an individual approval. This approval is issued by the supreme building authority of the respective federal

state and is valid for a specific construction project only. It cannot be transferred to other projects even if these are similar or even practically identical. However, the documentation used for obtaining the initial individual approval may be able to be used to apply for a further individual approval and thus simplify the whole procedure.

The content of the application is determined by the supreme building authority, and the test regime for the experimental investigations and the testing institute where these are to be carried out must be agreed in advance (Figs. 1 and 2). The nomination of a registered expert for any reports that may be required should also be agreed with the authorities beforehand. In principle, planners must contact the supreme building authority responsible at an early stage in order to agree on the procedure, the institutes that should be involved and the scope of the analyses, certification and component testing. In doing so, it is also possible to clarify whether any constructional changes are possible that might render certain tests superfluous, or whether relaxations in the verification procedure might be possible for certain forms of construction. The better the coordination with the authorities, the easier it is to minimise the time frame for the approval procedure. The applicant pays the costs of the procedure. Besides experimental investigations and reports, which will involve additional costs, supervision of the work on site may be called for within the scope of the approval. After submitting all the documentation required and obtaining a positive assessment from the supreme building authority, it is usually possible to obtain approval for a specific application. However, an individual approval is not a substitute for approval for the building as a whole, which has to be obtained in any case.

Experimental tests for glass constructions
The requirements of the building authorities in the individual federal states within the scope of the approval procedure may turn out to be different, but for some forms of glass construction the same tests are always required. Such tests must always be carried out on specimens that are identical with the original components with respect to glass configuration, support conditions and other factors. The number of test specimens is specified by the supreme building authority.

Pendulum impact tests for the experimental verification of the impact resistance of safety barrier glazing are carried out on at least two glazing assemblies that reproduce the original construction sufficiently accurately. The pendulum itself is in the form of a pair of tyres weighing 50 kg, which, depending on the form of the safety barrier construction, are swung against the glass from a height of 450, 700 or 900 mm to simulate the impact of a person on the glass (Figs. 4 and 5). In doing so, the pendulum may neither penetrate the glass nor dislodge it from its fixings. Glazing using laminated safety glass may not exhibit any cracks with apertures exceeding 76 mm and no fragments of glass are permmitted to fall out and endanger circulation zones. If it passes the TRAV tests, the safety barrier glazing is generally awarded a national test certificate. For glazing whose construction deviates significantly from the TRAV, however, pendulum impact tests must be carried out to prove the necessary impact resistance within the scope of a national technical approval or an individual approval.

Overhead glazing not covered by the provisions of the TRLV (Tab. T6) must be tested to establish its residual loadbearing capacity. To do this, glazing already

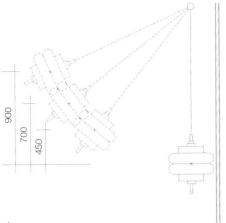

4

5

subjected to a uniformly distributed load must be struck in such a way that both panes of a laminated safety glass element are broken and an unfavourable crack pattern created. Afterwards, this totally damaged glazing must continue to carry the load for a certain period of time (which depends on the nature of the risk and the time taken to clear the danger area completely and cordon it off, but at least 24 hours) without failing completely and without any fragments falling out which could endanger the circulation zone below. The uniformly distributed load is applied, for example, by sacks filled with sand which are intended to simulate a snow load on the glass.

In the case of glazing for occasional foot traffic only, the tests on components should attempt to establish whether the glass component for walking on is able to carry the foot traffic load when the topmost pane of glass has failed due to an impact. This can happen when a person performing cleaning or maintenance work on the glass drops a heavy tool, for instance. How the construction reacts to the impact of a person falling on the glass must also be investigated. The test is in most cases carried out according to GS-BAU-18. In this test the pane of glass is tested with a 100 kg weight that is placed on an area measuring 200 × 200 mm, which is intended to simulate the weight of a person. The topmost pane of glass subjected to this load is subsequently destroyed. The weight is left on the totally damaged pane for 15 minutes. Afterwards, it is removed and an impact body is dropped onto the pane from a height of at least 1.2 m, to represent a falling person. The impact body in this case is a linen sack filled with glass beads and weighing 50 kg. After this impact body has struck the glass, it is replaced by the person-equivalent load, which again is left on the pane for

another 15 minutes. During the test, the glazing may neither slip out of its fixings nor be penetrated by the impact body, and no fragments of glass are allowed to fall out and endanger a circulation zone. In some cases, depending on the federal state, proof of loadbearing capacity for limited foot traffic must be established using the ball drop test (Fig. 3). Future regulations within the scope of the DIN 18008 series of standards will specify substituting the sack of glass beads by the pendulum as used in the safety barrier test.

Trafficable glazing must also exhibit adequate impact resistance and loadbearing behaviour after breakage, i.e. a residual loadbearing capacity. In this case a hard impact is simulated by a steel body weighing 40 kg, the top part of which is cylindrical, the bottom conical. This is allowed to fall from a height of 800 mm onto the pane of glass already subjected to half the intended imposed load in such a way that it causes maximum damage to the glass and its fixings. The imposed load consists of the weight of several persons (each 100 kg applied to an area measuring 200 × 200 mm) in an unfavourable loading arrangement. After passing the tests successfully, the totally damaged glazing is tested for its residual loadbearing capacity: the glass must remain in place for at least 30 minutes and no fragments are permitted to fall out and endanger a circulation zone below.

1   Loadbearing tests within the scope of an individual approval with three times the characteristic load on a section of a glass barrel vault for the roof to be added over an inner courtyard at the Reich President's Palace in Berlin. In order to carry the loads placed on the glass, the supporting steel members used here in the test are larger than the actual members that will be used for the real application.
2   Tests tailored to the particular needs of a construction project are often required within the scope of an individual approval. In the case of the roof over the inner courtyard to the Reich President's Palace in Berlin, it was buckling tests, carried out on the panes shown subjected to a uniformly distributed load in Fig. 1. The test had to establish which deformations ensue and at which compression load, introduced via the edge of the panes, the pane fails. The photograph shows the moment of complete failure of the insulating glass unit made from 8 mm toughened safety and laminated safety glass, the latter in turn made from 8 mm heat-strengthened glass and 19 mm toughened safety glass.
3   Ball drop test to DIN 52338 for testing laminated glass for quality control purposes with the glass holding assembly as specified in the standard. However, when using the ball drop test for testing for occasional foot traffic, the dimensions of the glass and the design of the supporting construction must correspond sufficiently accurately with the true construction. The steel ball is allowed to fall onto the glass from a defined height in order to destroy the pane, which afterwards must still carry a certain load.
4   Schematic presentation of the pendulum impact test. The drop height of 900 mm is used for category A safety barrier glazing, 700 mm for category B safety barrier glazing, and 450 mm for category C safety barrier glazing.
5   Impact body for pendulum impact test

Examples of the use of building with glass

Museum in Kansas City

Architects:	Steven Holl Architects, New York
	Steven Holl, Chris McVoy
Detailed design:	Berkebile Nelson Immenschuh McDowell Architects, Kansas
City Structural engineers:	Guy Nordenson & Associates, New York
Glass consultants:	R. A. Heintges & Associates, New York
Completed:	2007

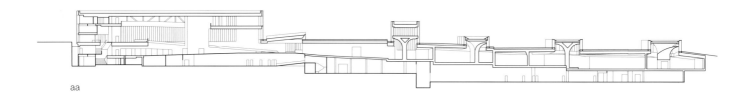

aa

Section · Plan
Scale 1:1500

1 Museum café
2 Upper entrance lobby
3 Void

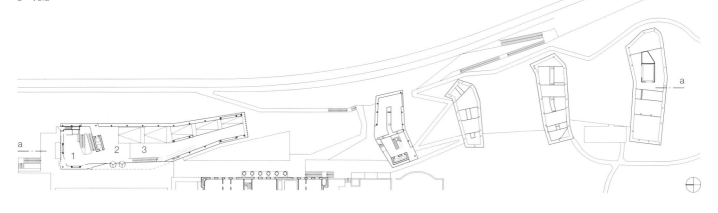

The elongated architectural landscape of this approx. 16 000 m² extension to the Nelson Atkins Museum is concealed to a large extent behind grassy banks. From the outside the new building with its five glass blocks rising out of the ground looks like a group of separate buildings surrounded by sculptures. But from the inside it is a coherent whole that tracks the topography of the landscape. And, once inside, it soon becomes clear that the T-shaped wall elements rounded off at the top, which the architect describes as optical lenses, are not just there to con-

ceal ventilation ducts or the steel structure supporting the roof. Instead, they are used to capture daylight and redirect it towards the darker areas of the interior. These glass facades consist of an outer leaf of translucent profiled glass elements and an inner leaf of single glazing. This double-leaf construction is not only advantageous from the building physics viewpoint; it also provides first-class protection against dangerous ultraviolet radiation. Direct sunlight is scattered, redirected, reflected, refracted or absorbed by the sand-blasted, etched or textured

glasses depending on position and time of day. Profiled glass normally has a greenish tint, but the iron oxide content responsible for this effect was significantly reduced for the glass of the Nelson Atkins Museum. The result is a radiant white glass enclosure which during the day creates a supernatural, mystical lighting effect, especially in the circulation zones directly behind the facade. A similar, but reversed, effect ensues when the glass blocks, conceived as "instruments of light", begin to glow like abstract sculptures as darkness falls.

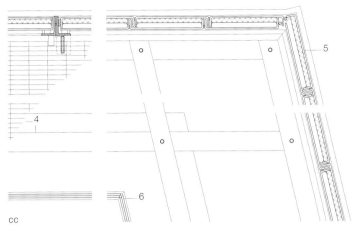

cc

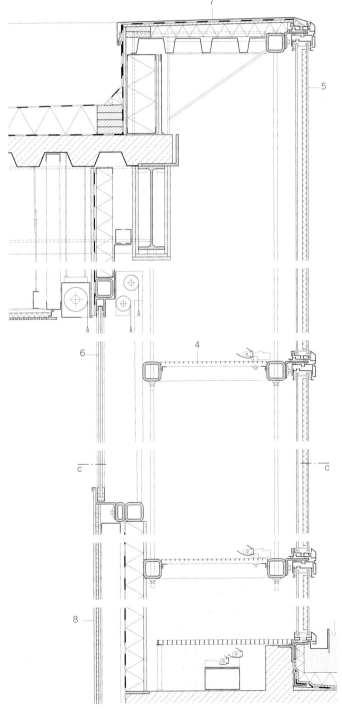

Horizontal section • Vertical section
Scale 1:20
4 Steel frame, galvanised, 25 mm, 100 × 100 mm
   square hollow sections
5 Profiled glass outer leaf, 57 × 400 × 10 mm,
   etched texture, reduced iron oxide content
   24 mm PMMA capillary inlay, coated
   27 mm air cavity, sand-blasted profiled glass inner
   leaf, 57 × 400 × 6 mm, reduced iron oxide content
   in 110 mm aluminium frame
6 Laminated safety glass, 2 No. 9.5 mm, etched on
   the inside
7 Sheet aluminium, 0.8 mm, waterproofing, 13 mm OSB
   75 mm rigid foam insulation, 2 layers
   75 mm steel trapezoidal profile sheeting
   65 mm steel T-section
8 Painted plasterboard, 12.5 mm
   12.5 mm plywood, 12.5 mm plasterboard
   92 mm steel channel posts
   vapour barrier, 92 mm glass fibre insulation
   16 mm plasterboard

Liesborn Abbey Museum

Architects: Baumewerd Architekten,
                     Münster
Structural engineers: Gantert und Wiemeler
                     Ingenieurplanung, Münster
Completed: 2004

A new building was required to supplement a church dating from the Middle Ages and a former Benedictine abbey built in the 18th century. There ist now a two-storey block that together with the community centre forms a new urban space where the monastery refectory once stood.

A two-level glazed bridge links the abbey's existing exhibition rooms with the monolithic new construction, facilitating a tour through all the rooms. Whereas the areas on the ground floor are reserved for temporary exhibitions, the upper floor houses a permanent collection of modern art. The basement contains depots, the archive and a plant room. In order to avoid having to compete with the exhibits on display, the design of the interior is sedate and straightforward. Dividing walls can be set up as required to create rooms of different sizes. A limited number of narrow, room-high windows, reminiscent of arrow-slits, allow beams of daylight to enter and visually break up the long interior. Heating pipes are incorporated in both the reinforced concrete floor slabs and the masonry walls. Backed up by the thermal mass of the solid external walls, this guarantees fairly constant interior climate conditions. The shimmering greenish outer skin of glass ceramic panels – completely covering the museum – is a homage to the patina of the copper roof on the church tower and the colouring of the window surrounds of the adjacent building. The main constituent in the 18 mm thick translucent elements is recycled, ground glass granulate. After melting, the glass solidifies into a crystalline structure with a three-dimensional look, with small inclusions and bubbles visible in the surface.

Section
Plans
Scale 1:400

1 Exhibition
2 Bridge
3 Archive
4 Plant room
5 Depot

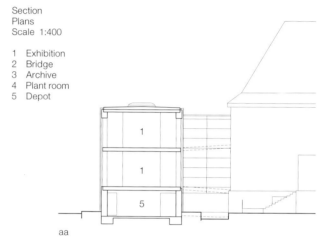

aa

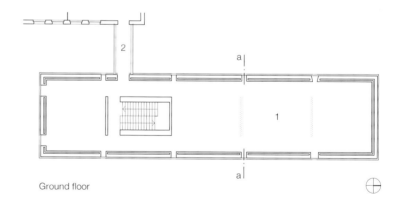

Ground floor

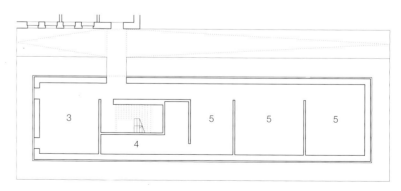

Basement

Horizontal section
Vertical section
Scale 1:20

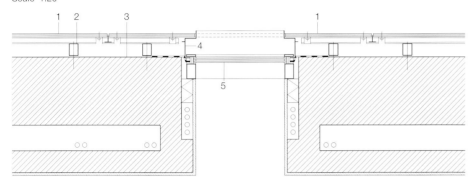

bb

1 Glass ceramic panels made from recycled glass, 18 mm
2 Aluminium supporting framework
3 Calcium silicate bricks, 360 mm
135 mm space for services
115 mm calcium silicate bricks
15 mm plaster
4 Sheet aluminium, painted, 3 mm
5 Insulating glass: 8 mm laminated safety glass + 16 mm cavity + 8 mm toughened safety glass
6 Aluminium profiled sheeting, 50 × 429 × 1 mm, fixed to 1.5 mm steel top-hat sections
180–260 mm mineral fibre insulation
vapour barrier
250 mm reinforced concrete
7 Peripheral strip lighting
8 Air inlet, perforated sheet aluminium, 3 mm

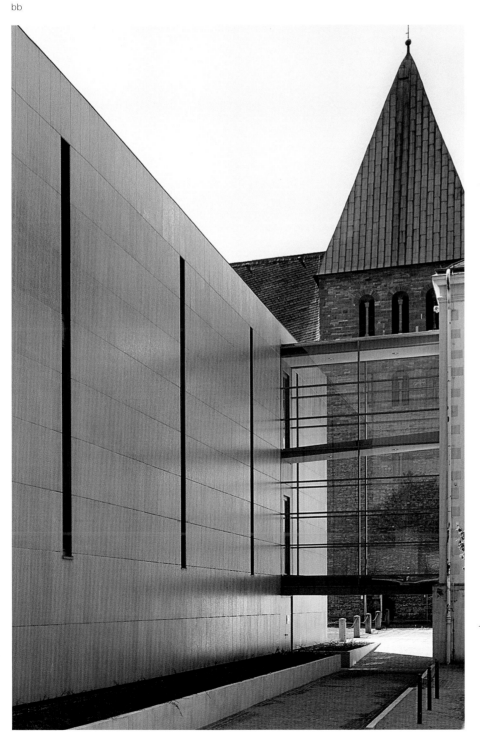

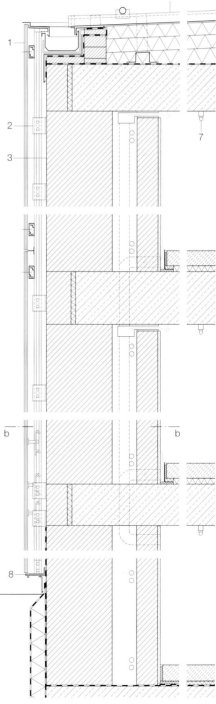

Mixed commercial and residential building in Aarau

Architects: Burkard, Meyer. Architekten, Baden
Urs Burkard, Adrian Meyer
Structural engineers: MWV Bauingenieure, Baden
Facade consultants: Ernst Schweizer AG, Hedingen
Completed: 2005

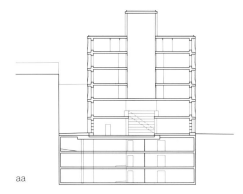

aa

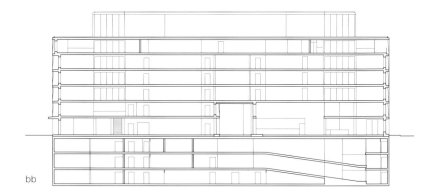

bb

A new "media building" for the AZ Medien Group, combining living and working under one roof, has been built between the railway station and the old part of the town. This six-storey block with its precisely configured outline fits seamlessly into its surroundings and, thanks to its glazed facade, appears surprisingly lightweight. At ground level there is a passage through the building, which is denoted by a widening on the east side and a return in the facade on the opposite side. The volume of the building is further broken up by two lightwells, which ensure that ample daylight reaches the interior. The striking feature of this building is its glass envelope; this is the visible outer leaf of a double-leaf facade and it divides the facade into storey-high horizontal bands. Depending on the lighting conditions, the inner leaf – a fenestrate facade clad with a wood-based panel product finished with a red-brown glaze – is either clearly visible or irritatingly veiled due to the reflections of the neighbouring buildings. The special effect of the glass envelope is achieved by the cranked glass panes. These were produced by heating the finished laminated glass panes, then passing them over a mould at a temperature of 600 °C and subsequently bonding them to rectangular frame members.

Sections · Plans
Scale 1:750

1 Bookshop
2 Access to apartments
3 Passage
4 Access to offices
5 Restaurant
6 Lightwell
7 Apartment
8 Loggia

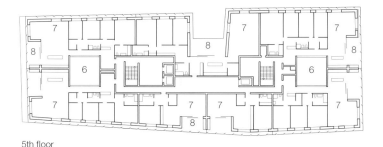

5th floor

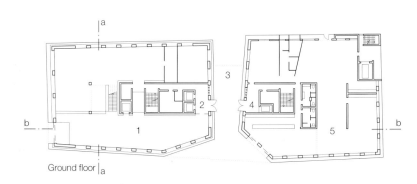

Ground floor

Horizontal section
Vertical section
Scale 1:20

9 Stainless steel square hollow
   section, 40 × 40 mm
10 Cranked laminated safety glass
   made from 2 No. 8 mm toughened
   safety glass
11 Ventilation flap, cement-bonded
   particleboard, red-brown opaque
   glaze finish
12 Cement-bonded particleboard,
   20 mm, red-brown opaque glaze
   finish
   ventilation cavity
   160 mm mineral wool insulation
   200 mm precast concrete element

   10 mm plaster
13 Cement-bonded particleboard,
   red-brown opaque glaze finish
14 Cover to heating, sheet steel, bent,
   perforated, painted
15 Trunking for heating pipes and
   electric cables
16 Precast concrete element with PUR
   liquid-applied waterproofing and
   quartz sand finish
17 Insulating glass: 8 mm toughened
   safety glass + 16 mm cavity + 8 mm
   toughened safety glass
18 Shelf, wood-based product, painted
19 Seamless mineral floor finish, 5 mm
   90 mm cement screed
   separating layer
   100 mm rigid XPS foam insulation
   reinforced concrete ground slab

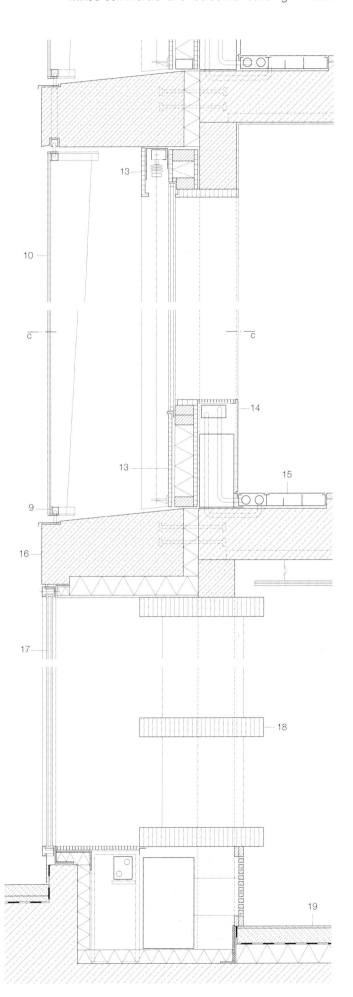

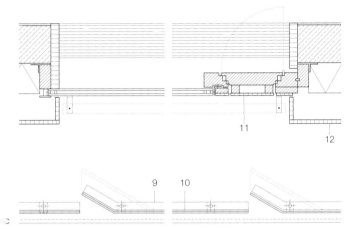

Production building in Hettenshausen

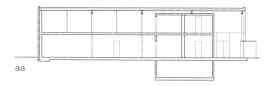

Architect: Peter Heilmaier, Munich
Structural engineers: CIP Ingenieure, Munich
Facade consultants: Glas & Metall Diemer,
                     Hettenshausen
Completed: 2000

The purpose behind this new production building on the edge of Hettenshausen, 45 km north of Munich, was to demonstrate the activities of the client – the manufacture and installation of glass facades, metal constructions and interior fitting-out – and permit the maximum involvement of the company itself in the construction. With that as his brief, the architect decided on a two-storey, flat-roofed shed with a steel frame and reinforced concrete core to ensure stability. A double-leaf reinforced concrete wall on the west side also contributes to the necessary overall stability and, at the same time, functions as a thermal mass. The building is glazed over its full height on the other three sides and demonstrates openness and transparency, with the manufacturing activities on the ground floor visible from outside. The offices and reception are on a mezzanine floor along the south facade, separated from the manufacturing bay by a glass dividing wall, which nevertheless enables direct visual contact and visual communication between the planning and production departments.

A modular grid of elements placed horizontally dominates the external appearance. To help reduce costs, the facade makes use of a standard facade system, although the posts have been omitted. The facade rails made from U140 steel channels are suspended on steel rods. These rods are welded to facade fins that transfer the loads to the perimeter members of the roof construction. The outer skin made from 1.70 × 1.09 m insulating glass units is only fixed to the facade rails with anodised aluminium glazing bars; the vertical joints are sealed. The entrance in the south-east corner fits into the structure of this facade: square in cross-section, its height is equal to two panes of glass and it is positioned centrally between the two southern-most bays.

Section · Plans
Scale 1:500

 1 Assembly shop
 2 Workshop
 3 Personnel facilities
    with changing room
    and WC
 4 Store
 5 Foyer
 6 Void
 7 Office
 8 Reception
 9 Corridor
10 Meeting room
11 Void

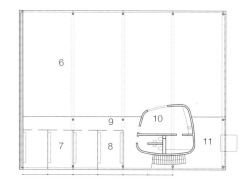

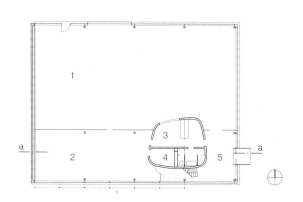

Horizontal section through facade and door
Vertical section through facade
Scale 1:20

12 Steel square hollow section, 60 × 60 mm
13 Sheet aluminium, 3 mm
14 Sliding glass door
15 Insulating glass, U-value = 1.1 W/m²K
16 Gravel topping, 50 mm
     waterproofing
     120 mm mineral wool insulation
     vapour barrier
     150 mm trapezoidal sheeting
17 Facade rail hanger, 16 mm steel rod
18 Roof beam, HEA 400
19 Steel circular hollow section, 219 dia. × 4.5 mm
20 Facade rail, 140 mm steel channel

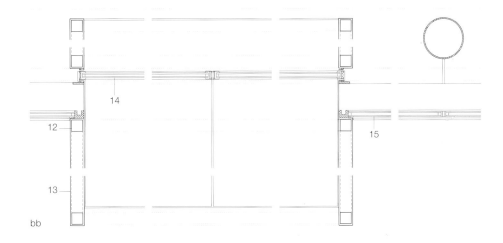

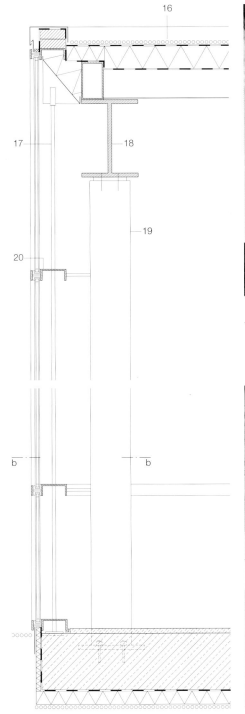

Glass museum in Toledo

Architects:	SANAA, Tokyo
	Kazuyo Sejima + Ryue Nishizawa
Detailed design:	Kendall Heaton Associates, Houston
Structural engineers:	SAPS – Sasaki & Partners, Tokyo
	Guy Nordenson & Associates, New York
Facade consultants:	Front. Inc., New York
Completed:	2006

Transparency is celebrated with this completely glazed enclosure to the new glass museum in Toledo. The pavilion-type construction, situated on the "Toledo Museum of Art" campus in the US state of Ohio, houses high-quality exhibitions, including one of the world's largest collections of glass. Besides the exhibition areas, this new building contains a glass-blowing studio, a hall for special events and a cafeteria.

As it was essential to integrate the glass pavilion very carefully into the park with its stock of old trees, the architects opted for a flat, single-storey structure; transparency and reflections tie the building into the landscape, its surroundings. Three glazed inner courtyards interrupt and illuminate the approximately square (57 × 62 m) plan form. Behind the glazed outer skin, organically shaped glass-walled rooms line up along the wide "promenade". Without corners, the rooms seem to flow into one another, the roof appears to float above. An impression of weightlessness is created by the minimised columns of white-painted steel and the solid wall elements of a few room capsules that support the roof. Every glass element was cut, bent and glued according to the specification in an elaborate process. Flush steel sections let into the floor and the roof with Teflon sealing strips fix the glass walls placed adjacent to each other and prevent restraint stresses in the glass. The voids between the glass walls function as climate buffer zones; the air-conditioning system installed in the roof space regulates the temperature and humidity in the rooms. Delicate, semi-transparent white curtains attenuate the incoming direct light and create an entrancing atmosphere.

Plan on roof structure
Scale 1:1500

Section · Plan
Scale 1:750

1 Foyer
2 Café
3 "Promenade"
4 Collection exhibits
5 Inner courtyard
6 Main exhibition
7 Relaxation area
8 Store
9 Hall for events
10 Glass-blowing studio
11 Toilets
12 Cloakroom
13 Glass workshop

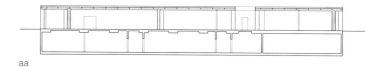

aa

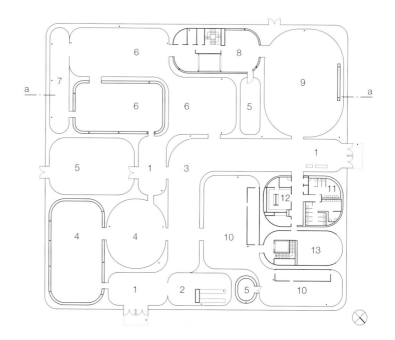

Vertical section
Scale 1:20

14 Waterproofing, 3 mm
    110–125 mm XPS thermal insulation
    2 mm vapour barrier
    50 × 50 × 2 mm trapezoidal profile
    sheeting
    IPE 255 steel roof beam
15 Steel beam, HEB 330
16 Sheet aluminium, 5 mm, anodised
    30 mm metal fixings
    3 mm waterproofing
    15 mm wood-based product
    fixed to
    40 mm insulated sheet metal panel
    2 mm vapour barrier
    300 × 80 × 20 mm perimeter steel
    channel

17 Steel angle, 190 × 80 × 12 mm
18 Thermal break, 280 × 60 mm,
    XPS in sheet steel
19 Radiant heaters
20 Steel angle, 110 × 80 × 10 mm,
    fixed to plate, 200 × 10 mm
21 Laminated safety glass,
    2 No. 10 mm,
    vertical joints sealed
22 Laminated safety glass,
    2 No. 13 mm
23 Acoustic plasterboard, 12 mm, white
24 Cement screed, 76 mm, polished,
    with underfloor heating
    2 mm separating layer
    reinforced concrete ground slab
25 Sheet metal cover, 2 mm
    steel angle base trim,
    250 × 50 × 10 mm

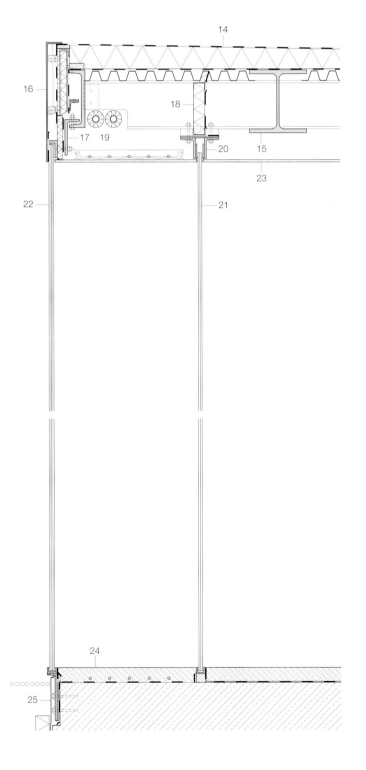

Overhead glazing to refectory and president's office at Technische Universität Dresden

Architects: Maedebach, Redeleit & Partner
Architekten, Dresden
Structural engineers: Leonhardt, Andrä & Partner,
planer: Dresden
Completed: 2007

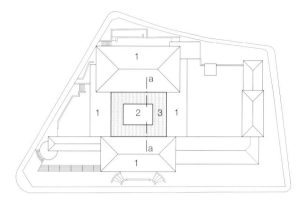

Location plan
Scale 1:2000
Section
Scale 1:400

1 Dining hall
2 Servery
3 Glass roof
4 Kitchen

Over the past 80 years, a heterogeneous group of buildings – in diverse styles and for a great variety of uses – has evolved on the campus of the Dresden University of Technology . Within the scope of a fundamental modernisation of the complex, it seemed obvious to optimise the refectory in terms of both its organisation and layout. An internal courtyard surrounded by four dining halls with a total of three serveries, not unlike a marketplace, presented a good opportunity for a new function. A gently sloping glass roof now spans more than 5.8 m from the external walls of the enclosing buildings to the flat roof of the new central servery.

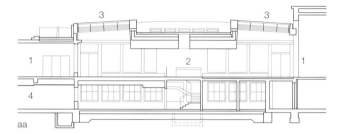

In order to achieve complete transparency, the architects – in close corporation with the structural engineers – designed a laminated safety glass loadbearing structure, which had to pass a loading test plus a 12-hour residual loadbearing capacity test in order to be granted an individual approval (ZiE). The main and transverse beams are arranged on a 1.45 m grid. This ensures that all beams have lateral restraint and prevents any damage spreading beyond the bays directly affected. For economic and visual reasons, all beams are 350 mm deep and connected via galvanised steel nodes. Important aspects in the design of these nodes were simple assembly and minimum dimensions so that the overall impression of transparency would not be unduly disturbed. The square panes of solar-control glass rest on linear supports and form a flat roof surface. The minimal roof pitch of 6° is sufficient to ensure sufficient water run-off (and hence a self-cleaning effect) between the glazing bars, which are only installed parallel with the slope. The total cost of the roof was similar to that of a conventional steel-and-glass construction.

Horizontal section
Vertical section
Scale 1:20

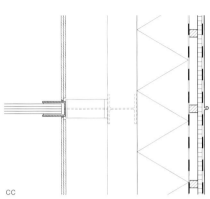

cc

5 Solar-control glass, fall 6 %; laminated safety glass: 2 No. 12 mm toughened safety glass + 16 mm cavity + 2 No. 12 mm heat-strengthened glass, g-value 36 %, light permeability 63 %, U-value 1.1 W/m^{2}K
6 Node, 8 mm sheet galvanised steel
7 Secondary beam, laminated safety glass: 4 No. 12 mm toughened safety glass
8 Steel post, HEA 160
9 Sheet zinc cladding with double welt joints separating layer

   24 mm timber sheathing
   50 mm air cavity
   waterproofing, PE sheeting, vapour-permeable
   240 mm mineral fibre insulation
   vapour barrier
10 Gravel topping
   bitumen waterproofing
   180–360 mm rigid foam insulation with integral falls
   vapour barrier
   250 mm reinforced concrete (existing)
11 Acoustic panel, 25 mm

12 Smoke and heat vent
13 Plasterboard, 2 No. 12.5 mm
14 Aluminium grille
15 Ventilation duct
16 Reconstituted stone flags to rooftop terrace, 40 mm
   on gravel bed
   bitumen waterproofing
   220 mm rigid foam insulation
   vapour barrier
   350 mm reinforced concrete

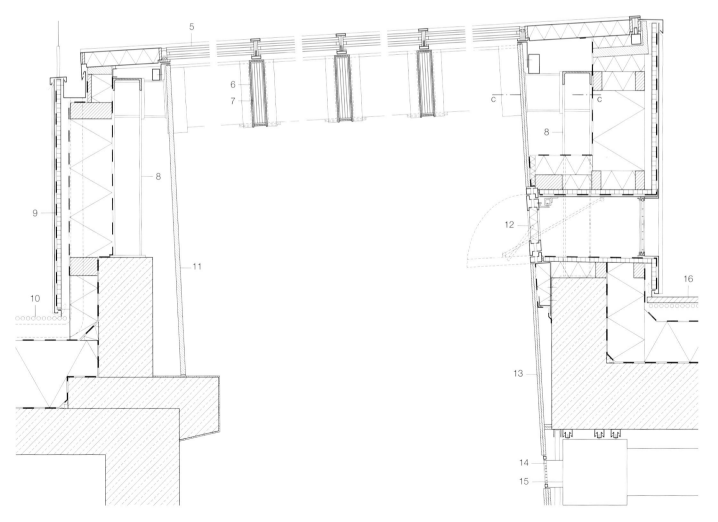

Concert pavilion "Schubert Club Band Shell" in Minnesota

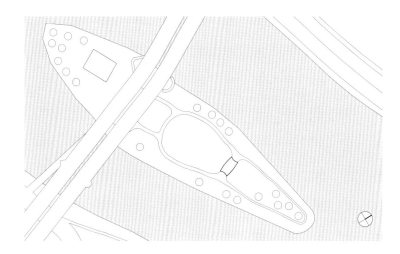

Architect: James Carpenter
                        Design Associates, New York
Structural engineers: Skidmore, Owings & Merrill
                        Engineering, Chicago
                        Schlaich Bergermann &
                        Partners, New York
Completed: 2002

The open-air stage, with its arched roof of glass and stainless steel on an island in the Mississippi, has become a new landmark in the city of St. Paul and creates a visual and acoustic framework for performances. Thanks to its anticlastic curvature and smooth glass covering, during the day the sunlight is reflected in different directions or permeates diffusely through the panes with their etched finish on the inside. At night appropriate illumination gives the structure a sculptural character.

The high snow loads in the northern USA determined the dimensions of the shell, and seasonal flooding demanded an open form and a stable, piled foundation. The piles support inclined precast concrete walls that transfer the thrust of the arch into the subsoil, where three transverse beams between the foundations resist the horizontal force of the steel arch and carry the load of the stage itself. The walls track the curved shape of the roof and there are two main rectangular arch beams. Between these, curved stainless steel tubes in two planes span in both directions to create a three-dimensional lattice with a bay size of 610 × 760 mm. There are also diagonal tie bars crisscrossing the entire structure. The shell is 7.6 m long and spans 15.2 m. The external geometry of the shell follows that of circle segments with a constant radius of curvature. This meant that standardised connection details could be used. It also limited the number of different panes of rectangular, flat glass. The panes are held in place at the corners by individual aluminium clamp fixings attached above the stainless steel framing on 19 mm spacers.

Location plan
Scale 1:4000
Sections · Plan
Scale 1:200

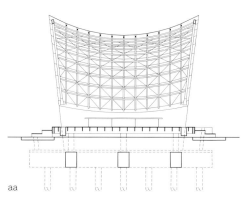

aa

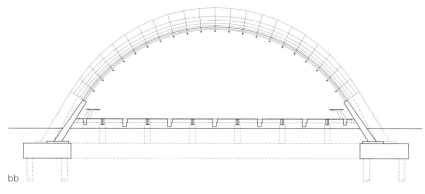

bb

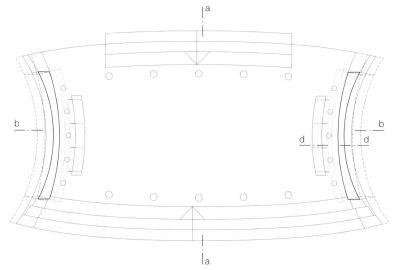

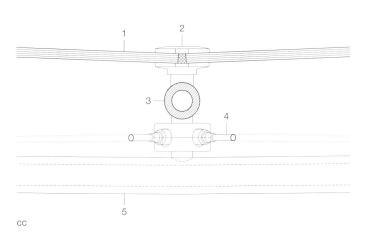

cc

Detail of node   Scale 1:5
Vertical section   Scale 1:50

1 Toughened clear glass panels: 6 mm float glass
   + 1.6 mm PVB interlayer + 6 mm float glass,
   outer surface clear, inner surface acid-etched
2 Aluminium individual clamp fixing
3 Longitudinal stainless steel tube, 48.3 mm dia.
4 Stainless steel tie, 8.4 mm dia.
5 Transverse stainless steel tube, 48.3 mm dia.
6 Continuous stainless steel baseplate, 12.7 mm,
   cast into reinforced concrete wall
7 Precast concrete wall
8 Bench, wooden planks on steel supports
9 Stage floor, wooden planks
10 Timber beam, 2 No. 50 × 300 mm
11 Timber beam, 50 × 200 mm
12 Built-in spotlights, 230 mm dia.
13 Reinforced concrete column, 300 × 300 mm
14 Transverse reinforced concrete beam
15 Foundation, reinforced concrete ground beam on
   324 mm dia. piles

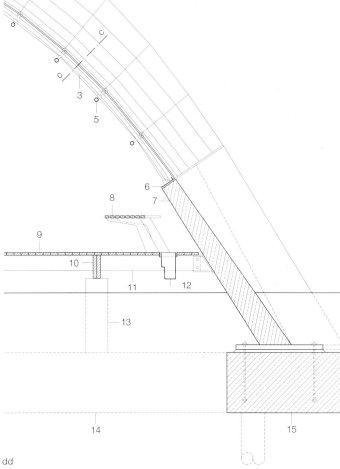

dd

Glass staircase in Paris

Architects: Kevin Roche, John Dinkeloo &
Associates, Hamden,
Connecticut
in cooperation with: SRA Architects, Chatillon,
and RFR, Paris
Specialist
consultants: RFR Ingenieure, Stuttgart
(structural engineering,
draft and final design)
Completed: 2006

This new headquarters for a building and telecommunications group is in the immediate vicinity of the Arc de Triomphe. The curving, all-glass staircase is located in a spacious atrium and links a non-public area on the ground floor with the meeting rooms on the first floor. On the outside, the steps are supported by a half-height glass balustrade, on the inside, by a storey-high glass wall. This 4.5 m high wall of curved panes of laminated safety glass, which are rigidly supported top and bottom on the reinforced concrete floor slabs, forms the backbone of the structural system. The

moderate temperature deformations are accommodated by bulging and the rotational freedom at the supports. The individual panes of glass are connected at the top of the construction by way of individual contact fixings in the joints and by a prestressed 6 mm stainless steel cable to form a shell structure. The dimensions of the fixings have been minimised to emphasize the transparent character of the staircase. The balustrade is secondary to the storey-high glass wall in structural terms and connected to this via the steps and stainless steel tubes fixed in the

joints with clamping discs. Another special feature of this staircase, in addition to the loadbearing structure, is its support for the steps themselves. The architects wished to avoid drilled holes and, instead, supported the steps on the narrow edge (just 15 mm wide) of the inner pane of the three-ply laminated glass, which was cut to follow the zigzag line of the steps. As this monolithic glass-and-steel composite construction was used for the first time in this application, a series of tests was required, similar to the individual approval procedure required in Germany.

Plan Scale 1:100
Section Scale 1:20
Detail Scale 1:5

1 Non-public zone
2 Atrium
3 Glass dividing wall
4 Balustrade, bent laminated safety glass made
   from 3 No. 15 mm float glass
5 Storey-high glass wall, laminated safety glass
   made from 3 No. 15 mm float glass
6 Balustrade upright, 60 × 35 mm rectangular
   hollow section
7 Handrail, 48 mm dia. stainless steel tube
8 Step, laminated safety glass,
   8 mm + 2 No. 15 mm + 8 mm,
   sand-blasted, non-slip top surface,
   joints filled with silicone to prevent slippage
9 Stainless steel individual clamp fixing
10 Stainless steel tie, 34 mm dia.
11 Polished stone, 20 mm, in 20 mm mortar bed
   45 mm screed, separating layer
   15 mm impact sound insulation
   300 mm reinforced concrete
12 Silicone joint
13 Stainless steel cover
14 Glass mounting, continuous,
   70 × 32 mm channel
15 Individual baseplates, 200 × 246 × 15 mm

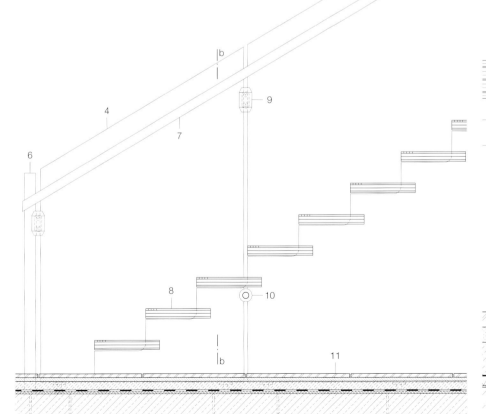

aa

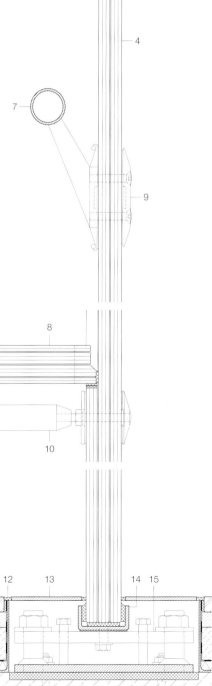

bb

99

Dutch embassy in Berlin

Architects: OMA, Office for Metropolitan
                      Architecture;
                      Rem Koolhaas, Rotterdam
Project partners: Ellen van Loon, Erik Schotte
Structural engineers: Royal Haskoning, Rotterdam
                      Arup, Berlin
Facade consultants: Rache & Willms, Aachen
                      Inside-Outside, Amsterdam
Completed: 2003

For their embassy in Berlin the Dutch selected a site on the banks of the River Spree with a view of passing river traffic and the riverside promenade – an environment that undoubtedly reminds the embassy staff of the canals of their own country. On the city side, the new complex is framed by an L-shaped block containing apartments for staff and part of the access arrangements. Bridges and ramps connect these "service" areas to the main body of the embassy. Only the ground floor was provided with bullet-resistant glass. The offices on the upper floors have a double-leaf facade made of separate elements, which acts as a "chimney" to carry away the exhaust air. To improve the rigidity of the elements at the corners of the building, the panes of glass were glued into their frames to act as structurally effective plates. The inner laminated safety glass panes can be opened for cleaning; narrow, opaque smoke vents have been incorporated between every second element, and these can also be opened for normal ventilation purposes. To provide privacy and shading, the outer laminated glass panes to the offices on the south facade were provided with a layer of expanded metal, which also lends the glazing a metallic sheen. Instead of a staircase, a corridor winds its way almost maze-like through the entire building, sometimes in the form of a ramp, sometimes as steps, leading up to the canteen. This corridor also acts as a "fresh-air duct" for the whole building. At the start of this corridor, where it runs along the outside of the building, the facade has been turned inside out, creating a glass ramp. At the level of the transparent fitness room, the corridor has been set back into the glass envelope by 400 mm. Here the insulating glass retreats to the inner leaf of the enclosing double-leaf facade; instead of side panels, glass fins provide the necessary stiffening.

Section · Plans
Scale 1:500

1 Garage
2 Main entrance
3 Foyer
4 "Fresh-air duct"
5 Hall for functions
6 Office
7 Conference room
8 Void
9 Apartment for embassy
  employee

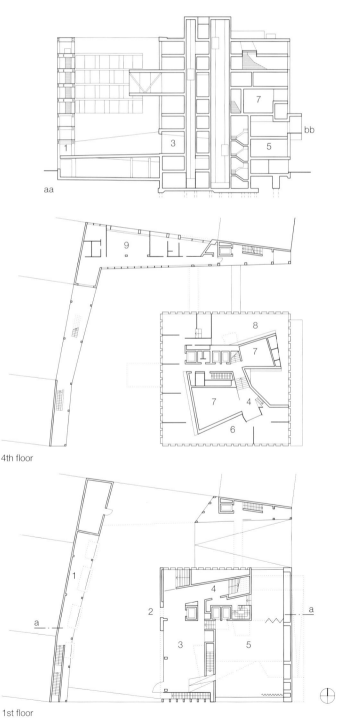

aa

4th floor

1st floor

Details of glass ramp
Scale 1:20

10 Outer pane of double-leaf facade element:
    6 mm toughened safety glass + 12 mm krypton-
    filled cavity + 6 mm toughened safety glass,
    U-value = 1.1 W/m²K, g-value = 0.28
11 Inner pane of double-leaf facade element:
    safety barrier of 12 mm laminated safety glass
    glued to peripheral frame, can be opened for
    cleaning
12 Sheet aluminium, polished silver anodised finish
13 Glazed safety barrier to ramp: 8 mm float glass +
    16 mm cavity + 16 mm laminated safety glass
    (2 No. toughened safety glass),
    U-value = 1.1 W/m²K
14 Top chord to suspended facade,
    160 × 20 mm steel flat

15 Facade post, 20 mm steel flat
16 Cover plate, 10 mm stainless steel
17 Thermal insulation, 30 mm unplasticised PVC
18 Bottom chord to facade, galvanised steel
19 Glass floor:
    wearing layer, 8 mm toughened safety glass,
    printed with dots to provide non-slip finish
    38 mm anti-bandit laminated safety glass
    40 mm air cavity
    green foil bonded to insulating unit
    8 mm float glass + 16 mm cavity +
    16 mm laminated safety glass
20 Silicone, black
21 Outlet for exhaust air from office
22 Built-in light fitting

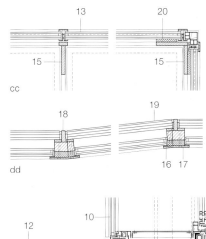

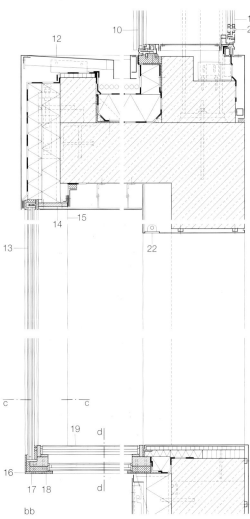

Glossary

Acoustic sheet
A plastic sheet used in → laminated glasses which owing to its chemical composition, tuned to certain frequency ranges, is able to improve the sound insulation.

Adhesion
Bonding forces between the surfaces of similar or dissimilar substances which are based on mechanical interlocking, physical interactions and chemical bonds.

Air side
The side of the pane of glass that is not in contact with the molten tin during the production of → float glass.

Anti-bandit glazing (anti-intruder, anti-vandal glazing)
Product based on → glass and/or plastics with a single- or multi-ply configuration having a uniform cross-section over the entire area of the anti-bandit layer(s). This type of glazing is generally transparent or light-permeable and provides a certain resistance to violent attack. The different types are allocated to different resistance classes: → glazing resistant to manual attack (thrown objects), → glazing resistant to manual attack (wielded objects), → bullet-resistant glazing, → blast-resistant glazing.

Anti-reflection glass
A glass product with a reduced reflectance in order to improve transparency and to avoid disturbing → reflections.

Bath side
The side of the pane of glass that is in contact with the molten tin during the production of → float glass.

Blast-resistant glazing
→ Glazing that can resist the pressure and effects of a certain blast wave.

Bonding of fragments
A necessary property of → laminated safety glass. Upon breakage, the fragments of glass are held together by the → PVB interlayer.

Borosilicate glass
→ Silica glass containing 7–15 % boron oxide. Used in the building industry in fire resistance applications.

Bowing and dishing effect
An optical effect caused by the convex and concave deflections of the individual panes of → multi-pane insulating glass. The cause is the relative change in the air pressure in the → cavity compared to that of its surroundings. The bowing and dishing effect is particularly evident in → reflections.

Brightness
Subjectively perceived luminance

Brittle failure
Sudden material failure with at best only minimal plastic deformation.

Bullet-resistant glazing
→ Glazing that impedes the penetration of projectiles fired from weapons.

Butt joint
A joint formed by gluing together two panes of glass either edge to edge or edge to face at any angle.

Casting resin
Clear intermediate material for → laminated glass that is applied as a liquid between the two panes to be joined and subsequently cures through exposure to heat or ultraviolet radiation.

Cavity
Hermetically sealed volume between two panes of a → multi-pane insulating glass unit.

CE marking
In the building industry the attestation of conformity for building products that may only be marketed and traded in accordance with European regulations.

Chemically toughened glass
A glass product strengthened by means of an ion exchange process (→ chemical toughening).

Chemical toughening
A method by way of which a compressive stress is generated in the surfaces of the glass by exchanging certain ions in the surface layer of the glass for those with a larger atomic radius. To achieve equilibrium of stresses, the compressive stress is balanced by a tensile stress in the core of the glass. The exchange of ions is carried out in an immersion process.

Clamp fixing
Point- or linear-type fastener that encloses the edge of the glass and hence supports the pane of glass without penetrating it by way of a → non-positive connection and a → positive connection.

Coating
Method for applying a layer of constant thickness to a glass product in order to modify the properties of the glass.

Cohesion
The inner strength of a substance that ensues through the interaction of forces of attraction between its atoms or molecules.

Cold working
The permanent elastic deformation of glass products at room or a slightly higher temperature by means of an external prestress. Usually involves the bending of → sheet glass panes about one axis in order to produce larger bending radii. See also → hot working.

Coloured glass
Types of glass that exhibit different spectral distribution of the → transmission, or re-emission, in the range of wavelengths of visible light.

Construction Products List (BRL)
This is published by the German Institute of Building Technology (DIBt) and contains the technical rules for building products and forms of construction. The BRL is made up of three lists, A, B and C. BRL A part 1: regulated building products. BRL A parts 2 and 3: building products (part 2) and forms of construction (part 3) that require an → AbP. BRL B: building products that may only be marketed and traded according to European regulations. BRL C: building products that do not require → verification of applicability.

Countersunk fixing
→ Point fixing that holds the pane of glass by being passed through a drilled – partly cylindrical, partly conical – hole.

Dichroic glass
A glass product with a coating of thin layers of oxide with different refractive indexes that creates a system of interference layers that split the incoming light into its spectral colours. The colour effects vary depending on lighting conditions, viewing angle and background.

Disc fixing
A component for the → point fixing of panes of glass which consists of two metal plates connected by a bolt or screw in a cylindrical hole drilled through the glass. The force transfer is by way of a → non-positive connection and a → positive connection.

Drawn sheet glass
Flat, transparent, colourless or tinted → sheet glass that is produced in a continuous, initially vertical, drawing process with fire-polished surfaces on both sides.

Edge cover
The amount of glass within a frame, determined by the distance between the edge of the pane and the structurally effective element of the frame or, for example, the → glazing bead.

Edge protection
Constructional measure for protecting the edges of glass against mechanical damage, the aim of which is to reduce the risk of failure of the pane concerned.

Edge seal
Peripheral, sealing, linear-type connection between two panes in a → multi-pane insulating glass unit.

Edge working
Improving the quality of a cut edge with respect to appearance, dimensional accuracy and strength by way of grinding and polishing.

Enamelling
The application of coloured ceramic inks to a glass product, which is permanently baked into the glass during the toughening process. Can be used over the entire surface or just part thereof (→ silk-screen printing).

ETAG
European Technical Approval Guideline (information for issuing a → European Technical Approval).

Etching
Removing the surface of the glass with an acid (normally hydrofluoric acid). The aim of this is typically to provide a matt finish (→ obscured glass) or for decorative purposes or to create a → non-slip surface.

European Technical Approval (ETA)
→ Verification of applicability for non-regulated building products or forms of construction issued on a European level.

Extra-clear glass
A type of → glass with a very low iron oxide content which does not exhibit the typical greenish tinge of normal glass.

Fire-resistant glazing
Component with one or more light-permeable elements that is fitted into a frame with fixings plus seals and fasteners prescribed by the manufacturer and complies with the requirements of DIN 4102-13, section 6. All these construction elements together, including the prescribed dimensions and tolerances, constitute the fire-resistant glazing.

Flashed glass
A type of → glass that consists of a backing glass and a thinner facing of, for example, → coloured glass or → opal glass.

Float glass
Flat, transparent, colourless or tinted → sheet glass with parallel and fire-polished surfaces produced by means of continuous casting on and flowing over a bath of molten metal.

Fusing glass
Suitable coloured → sheet glasses with coordinated expansion properties that are melted in a furnace at approx. 790–900 °C.

Gasket sealing
The sealing of windows and facades by way of preformed elastic sealing profiles to prevent ingress of water and ensure airtight joints.

Glass
Inorganic non-metallic material that is obtained through the complete melting of a mixture of raw materials at high temperatures, which produces a homogeneous fluid that is cooled to a solid state, normally without crystallisation.

Glass block (glass brick)
A glass product produced by pressing which consists of two parts that are fused firmly together airtight.

Glass ceramics
These products are manufactured like glass and upon cooling initially solidify to form → glass. However, subsequent heat treatment turns this into an essentially crystalline material. Due to this conversion process, glass ceramics have properties that deviate from those of glass.

Glass treatments
This is the general term for all further and secondary processes carried out on the basic glass products. It includes mechanical working (grinding, drilling), thermal treatment (bending, → toughening), surface treatments, → chemical toughening and processing to form → laminated glass, → laminated safety glass or → multi-pane insulating glass.

Glazing
General term for a unit consisting of panes of glass, glass fixings, seals and other ancillary items.

Glazing bead
Removable retaining member for the pane of glass which forms part of the glazing system.

Glazing for constant foot traffic
→ Horizontal glazing to which people (including the public) have permanent access and which is intended to form part of a circulation zone.

Glazing for occasional foot traffic
→ Overhead glazing that must satisfy certain requirements because it is walked on for the purpose of cleaning, maintenance and/or repairs.

Glazing resistant to manual attack (thrown objects)
→ Glazing that impedes the penetration of thrown or catapulted objects.

Glazing resistant to manual attack (wielded objects)
→ Glazing that delays the creation of an opening (breaking in/out).

Gluing
Method of jointing in which the components cannot be dismantled afterwards because of → adhesion and → cohesion.

Heat-soaked toughened safety glass
→Toughened safety glass that has passed the → heat soak test and therefore has a much lower risk of → nickel sulphide failure.

Heat soak test
Hot storage of → toughened safety glass in order to eliminate panes with nickel sulphide inclusions (which shatter).

Heat-strengthened glass
A type of glass with increased resistance to mechanical and thermal stresses, achieved by way of thermal treatment, which, however, does not achieve the strength values of → toughened safety glass and has a fracture pattern similar to that of → float glass.

Horizontal glazing
General designation for → overhead glazing at an angle < 10° to the horizontal.

Hot working
For glass in building this is the plastic shaping method at temperatures above the transformation point (normally approx. 600 °C).

Hue
An optically effective property of → glass with a relatively high selective absorptance and non-diffuse light transmission. The view through the glass takes on a coloured appearance (→ coloured glass) but is still in focus. See also → obscuring.

Inclined glazing (sloping glazing)
→ Overhead glazing at an angle > 10° to the horizontal.

Individual approval (ZiE)
In Germany a unique → verification of applicability for a non-regulated building product or form of construction issued by the supreme building authority responsible.

Interference colours
Optical phenomenon caused by the superimposition of electromagnetic radiation with different wavelengths at one point. It manifests itself by splitting visible light into its spectral colours. This happens with glass in building primarily when several panes of → float glass are placed directly behind and parallel to one another.

Laminated glass
A product consisting of at least two panes of → glass connected by at least one intermediate layer of plastic. A plastic glazing material may be used as an alternative.

Laminated safety glass
A → laminated glass in which, in the case of breakage, the intermediate layer retains the fragments of glass, limits the size of any openings that may ensue, offers a residual strength and reduces the risk of injuries.

Lead glass
→ Silica glass with a lead oxide content > 10 %. Lead glass is used in optics and for shielding against x-rays.

Linear-type support
Continuous line bearing that can be on one, two, three or four sides, also in combination with point-type supports. An alternative to → point-type support.

List of Technical Construction Regulations (LTB)
The LTB contains technical rules for planning, designing and constructing buildings and structures and parts thereof and is implemented in each German federal state on the basis of the Model List of Technical Construction Regulations (MLTB).

Low E (emissivity) glass
A → sheet glass or sheet glass combination that owing to its selective absorption and → reflection properties guarantees reduced heat transmission and reduced heat emission.

Material bond
Irreversible jointing of parts that are held together by atomic and molecular forces consisting of → adhesion and → cohesion. Material bond jointing methods include welding, soldering and → gluing.

Model Building Code (MBO)
A building legislation document that each individual German state implements in the form of its Federal State Building Regulations (LBO).

Multi-pane insulating glass
A glazing unit consisting of a least two panes of glass that are separated by at least one → cavity filled with gas or air. At the edges the panes are connected by an airtight/gastight and moisture-resistant organic seal (→ edge seal).

National technical approval (AbZ)
In Germany a → verification of applicability for non-regulated building products or forms of construction issued by the German Institute of Building Technology (DIBt).

National test certificate (AbP)
In Germany a → verification of applicability that is used as an alternative to the → AbZ when the non-regulated building product or form of construction concerned can be assessed according to acknowledged test methods and their use is not connected with the fulfilment of significant building safety requirements (given in Construction Products List A parts 2 and 3). The AbP is issued by an accredited testing institute.

Nickel sulphide failure
A type of failure that occurs with → toughened safety glass due to the increase in volume of the nickel sulphide trapped within the glass.

Non-positive connection
Method of jointing in which the application of a force guarantees that the connection remains intact. Clamped, screwed and bolted connections are among this type.

Non-slip surface
The property of a floor covering (here also → glazing for occasional foot traffic, → glazing for constant foot traffic) to resist slipping.

Obscured glass
A glass product with a consistently roughened surface that scatters the light diffusely. The roughening can be achieved by way of → etching or → sand-blasting, in some cases by grinding.

Obscuring
→ Transmission with a diffuse passage of radiation. The view through is unfocused and blurred. See also → translucency.

Offline coating
A coating method that is carried out directly after the manufacture of the → sheet glass, primarily after → float glass production.

Online coating
A coating method that is carried out during → float glass production, directly on the hot ribbon of glass.

Opacity
Designation for a material's impermeability to light. The → transmittance of an opaque material is zero.

Opal glass
This type of → glass (also available coloured) is produced by adding fluorine compounds, phosphates or tin oxide to the melt.

Overhead glazing
→ Glazing at an angle > 10° to the vertical. This installation situation calls for special safety measures.

Patent glazing bar
A framing section mainly used for → linear-type support which connects the pane of glass to the supporting construction by means of contact pressure.

Patterned glass
Flat, translucent, colourless or tinted → sheet glass, manufactured by means of continuous casting and rolling.

Plate glass
1) Deprecated name for → float glass.
2) Up until the widespread use of the float glass process this was the usual term for high-quality, relatively distortion-free and transparent flat glass produced by rolling or drawing the ribbon of glass plus subsequent grinding and polishing.

Point fixing
General term for individual glass fasteners that are either in the form of a U-shaped component enclosing the edge of the glass through a positive connection (→ clamp fixing) or make use of a drilled holes, e.g. → disc fixing, → undercut anchor and → countersunk fixing.

Point-type support
Supporting the pane of glass at individual points either on the perimeter of the glass by way of clamping or within the area of the glass by way of fixings in drilled holes. An alternative to → linear-type support.

Polyvinyl butyral (PVB) interlayer
A viscoelastic film that is used as an intermediate layer when producing → laminated safety glass in order to retain the fragments of glass, limit the size of any openings, offer some residual loadbearing capacity and reduce the risk of injuries in the case of breakage.

Positive connection
Method of jointing in which the force transfer is achieved by way of the interlocking of the components.

Pressed glass
A glass product that is produced by pressing a smooth die into a mould with, generally, some form of profiling or contouring. Compressed air can be used as an alternative. → Glass blocks are pressed products.

Profiled glass (channel glass)
A translucent, colourless or tinted → soda-lime-silica glass, with or without wire inlay, produced by continuous casting and rolling and bent into a U-shape during manufacture.

Quartz glass
Colourless transparent and heat-resistant single-component glass with a silicon dioxide content > 99.5 %.

Rebate
Type of joint in a frame for holding and sealing a pane of glass. See also → setting blocks.

Redundancy
A design principle that increases the functional safety of a system by including additional parts or loadbearing reserves that in the normal case are not required. A structural system is redundant when after the failure of one part other parts carry the loads.

Refining
The removal of bubbles and dissolved gases from the glass melt, and homogenising during the melting process.

Reflection
In optics reflection is the rebounding of the light at the boundary surfaces of two neighbouring media. The angle of incidence, the surface properties, the wavelength, polarisation and the material properties all affect the nature and magnitude of the reflection.

Residual loadbearing capacity
The property of a glass element to be able to carry certain loads even after breakage.

Residual stability
The property of a glass element to remain in position and not fall after breakage.

Ribbon size
The maximum width of the → float glass, i.e. 3.21 m, which results from the manufacturing process and is normally combined with lengths of 4.50, 5.10 or 6.0 m.

Rolled glass
→ Patterned glass

Safety and security glasses
→ Sheet glass that, for example, reduces the risk of injury in the case of breakage, acts as a safety barrier or provides protection against attacks. We distinguish between → toughened safety glass and → laminated safety glass depending on the configuration and the safety or security specification.

Safety barrier glazing
→ Vertical glazing, loadbearing glass balustrades and spandrel panels and balustrade infill panels made from → glass that prevent persons from falling sideways and/or to a lower level.

Sand-blasting
A subtractive glass surface treatment that is employed for obscuring (→ obscured glass), labelling and decorative purposes.

Sealing compound
A substance used for the airtight and watertight closure of joints between similar or dissimilar materials.

Self-cleaning glass
A glass product with a dirt-repellent coating, the effect of which is to make it difficult for dirt and dust to cling to the surface, thus allowing rainwater to wash it off.

Setting blocks
Components, made from plastic or another suitable material, for positioning the pane of glass in a frame and transferring the forces to the supporting construction. We distinguish between setting and location blocks depending on the function.

Sheet glass
General term for all relatively thin, flat and bent panes of glass with essentially parallel surfaces.

Silica glass
→ Glass in which silicon dioxide is the main constituent. This is by far the most common type of glass produced, and includes → lead glass and → borosilicate glass.

Silk-screen printing
The application of coloured ceramic inks to parts of the surface of the glass product which are permanently baked into the surface during the toughening process. Templates can be used to create patterns and pictures.

Single glazing
→ Glazing that consists of only one pane of → sheet glass (also a pane of → laminated glass).

Soda-lime-silica glass
A type of glass that besides a high content of silicon dioxide also contains smaller proportions of sodium oxide, calcium oxide, magnesium oxide and aluminium oxide. This is the type of glass used most often in the building industry.

Solar-control glass
→ Sheet glass or sheet glass combination that owing to its absorption and → reflection properties provides protection against solar radiation (glass with increased heat radiation and light absorption and/or reflection).

Sound insulating glass
A → multi-pane insulating glass consisting of two or more panes of glass with coordinated thicknesses and cavities filled with air or a special gas mixture. → Laminated glass with an organic interlayer can also be used.

Structural sealant glazing (SSG)
A type of facade construction in which the panes of glass are connected to the supporting construction permanently by way of a loadbearing and sealing silicone adhesive to create a flush external surface without framing members.

Thermal toughening
Heating a glass product to a temperature of about 650 °C and subsequent abrupt cooling results in compressive stresses in the surfaces that are balanced by tensile stresses within the body of the glass due to the surfaces of the glass cooling faster than the core of the glass.

Toughened glass
A glass product with artificially generated compression zones at the glass surfaces and a tension zone within the body of the glass. The prestress is achieved by quenching temperatures in the viscoelastic range (→ thermal toughening) or by ion exchange (→ chemical toughening).

Toughened safety glass
Sheet glass that has undergone heat treatment to provide it with a greater resistance to mechanical and thermal stresses and which shatters into a multitude of blunt pieces (dice) upon breakage.

Translucency
An optical property of diffusely transmitting substances. The passage of the light beams is scattered at the rough – and hence matt-looking –surface and/or within the material. The view through is unclear and blurred. However, the transmittance of a translucent material need not necessarily be lower than that of a transparent one.

Transmission
Designation for the permeability of a medium with respect to electromagnetic waves. The ratio between the incident and transmitted components is called the transmittance. In glass used in building work the transmittance for radiation in the wavelength spectrum between infrared and ultraviolet is especially important.

Transparency
The term transparency is used differently depending on context. In the building industry a transparent component is one that exhibits a very high transmittance for a non-diffuse radiation passage. The view through is clear and focused.

Ü-mark
German designation for building products according to Construction Products List A part 1 that do not deviate or do not deviate significantly from the technical rules (regulated building products).

Undercut anchor
→ Point fixing that holds the pane at a discrete point via a hole drilled in only one side of the pane.

Unsupported edge
General expression for a visible, unprotected edge of a pane of glass without any support.

Verification of applicability
Required when using non-regulated building products or forms of construction. → AbZ, → ETA, → AbP or → ZiE documents are classed as suitable verification.

Vertical glazing
→ Glazing at an angle < 10° to the vertical.

Window
Opening in a lateral enclosing surface to an interior that permits the entry of daylight.

Wired glass, patterned wired glass
Flat, translucent, colourless or tinted → sheet glass that is produced by continuous casting and rolling and into which a mesh of steel wires, welded at every intersection, is inserted during production. The surfaces may be smooth or textured.

Appendix

Standards, directives, statutory instruments and recommendations (selection)

Anforderungen an begehbare Verglasungen; Empfehlungen für das Zustimmungsverfahren, Mar 2000 ed. In: Mitteilungen DIBt Feb 2001, pp. 60–62
Arbeitsstätten Richtlinie (ASR) 7/1: Sichtverbindung nach außen. Jun 1998
Arbeitsstätten Richtlinie (ASR) 8/4: Lichtdurchlässige Wände. Feb 1977
Bauregelliste A, Bauregelliste B, Liste C. 2008/1 ed. DIBt Mitteilungen, Sonderheft No. 36, Ernst & Sohn, Berlin, 2008
BGR 181 (Berufsgenossenschaftliche Regeln für die Sicherheit und Gesundheit bei der Arbeit): Fußböden in Arbeitsräumen und Arbeitsbereichen mit Rutschgefahr. Rev. ed., Oct 2003
DIN 18008 (draft standard) Glass in building – Design and construction rules, parts 1 to 7
E DIN 51131 Testing of floor coverings – Determination of the anti-slip property – Method for measurement of the sliding friction coefficient. Aug 2008
ETAG 002 Structural Sealant Glazing Systems, parts 1 to 3
DIN 4102 Fire behaviour of building materials and building components, parts 1, 4 and 13
DIN 4108 Thermal insulation and energy economy in buildings
DIN 4109 Sound insulation in buildings
DIN 4426 Equipment for building maintenance – Safety requirements for workplaces and access – Design and execution. Sept 2001
DIN 4243 Betongläser – Anforderungen, Prüfung. Mar 1978
DIN 5031-3 Optical radiation physics and illuminating engineering; quantities, symbols and units of illuminating engineering. Mar 1982
DIN 5034 Daylight in interiors, parts 1 and 2
DIN 18175 Glasbausteine – Anforderungen, Prüfung. May 1977
DIN 18516-4 Back-ventilated, non-loadbearing, external enclosures of buildings, made from tempered safety glass panels; requirements and testing. Feb 1990
DIN 51130 Testing of floor coverings – Determination of the anti-slip properties – Workrooms and fields of activities with slip danger, walking method – Ramp test. Jun 2004
DIN EN 356 Glass in building – Security glazing – Testing and classification of resistance against manual attack. Feb 2000
DIN EN 357 Glass in building – Fire resistant glazed elements with transparent or translucent glass products – Classification of fire resistance. Sept 2007
DIN EN 410 Glass in building – Determination of luminous and solar characteristics of glazing. Dec 1998
DIN EN 572 Glass in building – Basic soda-lime-silicate glass products, parts 1 to 9
DIN EN 673 Glass in building – Determination of thermal transmittance (U-value) – Calculation method. Jun 2003
DIN EN 1051 Glass in building – Glass blocks and glass pavers, parts 1 and 2
DIN EN 1063 Glass in building – Security glazing – Testing and classification of resistance against bullet attack. Jan 2000
DIN EN 1096 Glass in building – Coated glass, parts 1 to 4
DIN EN 1279 Glass in building – Insulating glass units, parts 1 to 6
DIN EN 1363-1 Fire resistance tests – Part 1: General requirements. Oct 1999
DIN EN 1364-1 Fire resistance tests on non-loadbearing elements – Part 1: Walls. Oct 1999
DIN EN 1365-1 Fire resistance tests on loadbearing elements – Part 1: Walls. Oct 1999
DIN EN 1748-1 Glass in building – Special basic products – Borosilicate glasses, parts 1-1 and 1-2
DIN EN 1748-2 Glass in building – Special basic products – Glass ceramics, parts 2-1 and 2-2
DIN EN 1863 Glass in building – Heat strengthened soda-lime-silicate glass, parts 1 and 2
DIN EN 12150 Glass in building – Thermally toughened soda-lime-silicate safety glass, parts 1 and 2
DIN EN 12337 Glass in building – Chemically strengthened soda-lime-silicate glass, parts 1 and 2
DIN EN 12354-3 Building acoustics – Estimation of acoustic performance of buildings from the performance of elements – Part 3: Airborne sound insulation against outdoor sound. Sept 2000
DIN EN 13024 Glass in building – Thermally toughened borosilicate safety glass, parts 1 and 2
DIN EN 13031-1 Greenhouses – Design and construction – Part 1: Commercial production greenhouses. Sept 2003
DIN EN 13124 Windows, doors and shutters – Explosion resistance; Test method, parts 1 and 2
DIN EN 13501 Fire classification of construction products and building elements, parts 1 and 2
DIN EN 13541 Glass in building – Security glazing – Testing and classification of resistance against explosion pressure. Feb 2001
DIN EN 14178 Glass in building – Basic alkaline earth silicate glass products, parts 1 and 2
DIN EN 14321 Glass in building – Thermally toughened alkaline earth silicate safety glass, parts 1 and 2
DIN EN 14449 Glass in building – Laminated glass and laminated safety glass – Evaluation of conformity/Product standard. Jul 2005
DIN EN 20140 Acoustics; measurement of sound insulation in buildings and of building elements, parts 2 and 10
DIN EN ISO 140-1 Acoustics – Measurement of sound insulation in buildings and of building elements, parts 1, 3 and 5
DIN EN ISO 717-1 Acoustics – Rating of sound insulation in buildings and of building elements – Part 1: Airborne sound insulation. Nov 2006
DIN V 11535-1 (pre-standard) Greenhouses, parts 1 + 2
GS-BAU-18 Grundsätze für die Prüfung und Zertifizierung der bedingten Betretbarkeit oder Durchsturzsicherheit von Bauteilen bei Bau- oder Instandhaltungsarbeiten. Feb 2001 ed.
GUV-SI 8027 Mehr Sicherheit bei Glasbruch. GUV-Informationen Sicherheit bei Bau und Einrichtung. Pub. by Bundesverband der Unfallkassen, Munich, Sept 2001
Musterbauordnung (MBO). Nov 2002 ed., Informationssystem Bauministerkonferenz, Berlin, 2002
Muster-Liste der Technischen Baubestimmungen (MLTB), Feb 2008 ed., Informationssystem Bauministerkonferenz, Berlin, 2008.
Technische Regeln für die Verwendung von absturzsichernden Verglasungen (TRAV); Jan 2003 ed.
Technische Regeln für die Verwendung von linienförmig gelagerten Verglasungen (TRLV); Aug 2006 ed.
Technische Regeln für die Bemessung und Ausführung von punktförmig gelagerten Verglasungen (TRPV); Aug 2006 ed.
Technische Richtlinien des Glaserhandwerks, Nos. 1–20, 8th ed., Verlagsanstalt Handwerk GmbH, Düsseldorf, 2004
Überkopfverglasungen im Rahmen von Zustimmungen im Einzelfall. Memorandum, Baden-Württemberg Building Technology Office. Apr 2008
Baden-Württemberg Ministry of the Economy (ed.): Bauen mit Glas. Informationen für Bauherren, Architekten und Ingenieure. Stuttgart, 2002

Bibliography

Baum, M.: Ulice na konci světa. O architektuře ajiných věcech – Straße am Ende der Welt. Über Architektur und andere Dinge. Akademie výtvarných umění – Akademie der Bildenden Künste/Kant, Karel Kerlický. Prague, 2007

Bell, M., Kim, J. (ed.): Engineered Transparency. The Technical, Visual, and Spatial Effects of Glass. Princeton Architectural Press, New York, 2009

Bolze, M.: Brandschutz im Glasbau. In: Weller, B. (ed.): glasbau2004. Proceedings, Institute of Building Construction, Technische Universität Dresden, Dresden, 2004, pp. 39–49

Bos, F., Louter, C., Veer, F.: Challenging Glass. Conference on Architectural and Structural Applications of Glass. Faculty of Architecture, Delft University of Technology. IOS Press BV, Amsterdam, 2008

Bos, F., Veer, F.: Consequence-based safety requirements for structural glass members. In: Glass Performance Days Tamglass Ltd. Oy: Glass Performance Days. 10th International Conference on Architectural and Automotive Glass. Glass Performance Days Ltd. Oy, Tampere, 2007, pp. 57–61

Bucak, Ö., Schuler, C.: Glas im Konstruktiven Ingenieurbau. In: Kuhlmann, U. (ed.): Stahlbaukalender 2008. Ernst & Sohn, Berlin, 2008, chap. 10, pp. 829–938

Compagno, A.: Intelligent Glass Facades. 4th ed., Birkhäuser, Basel, 1999

DuBois, M.: Glass bearing walls – a case study. In: Glass Performance Days Tamglass Ltd. Oy: Glass Performance Days. 10th International Conference on Architectural and Automotive Glass. Glass Performance Days Ltd. Oy, Tampere, 2007, pp. 179–183

Engel, H.: Tragsysteme. Structure Systems; 3rd ed., Hatje Cantz Verlag, Ostfildern, 2007

Fröhler, A.: Lexikon für Glas und Glasprodukte. Verlag Hofmann, Schorndorf, 2005

Ganslandt, R., Hofmann, H.: Handbuch der Lichtplanung. ERCO Leuchten GmbH Lüdenscheid, Vieweg & Sohn, Braunschweig/Wiesbaden, 1992

Glocker, W.: Glastechnik. C. H. Beck'sche Verlagsbuchhandlung, Munich, 1992

Gregory, R. L.: Auge und Gehirn. Psychologie des Sehens. Rowohlt Taschenbuch Verlag, Reinbek, 2001

Hagl, A.: Kleben im Glasbau. In: Kuhlmann, U. (ed.): Stahlbaukalender 2005. Ernst & Sohn, Berlin, 2005, chap. 8, pp. 819–861

Hecht. E.: Optik; 4th ed., Oldenbourg Wissenschaftsverlag, Munich, 2005

Herzog, T., Krippner, R., Lang, W.: Facade Construction Manual; 1st ed., Institut für Internationale Architektur-Dokumentation, Munich, 2004

Hoegner, H.: Glasbemessung. Bauaufsichtliche Regelungen. In: Weller, B. (ed.): glasbau2008; Proceedings. Institute of Building Construction, Technische Universität Dresden, Dresden, 2008, pp. 35–54

Institution of Structural Engineers: Structural use of glass in buildings. Structural Engineers Trading Organisation Ltd, London, 1999

Knaack, U.: Konstruktiver Glasbau. Rudolf Müller Verlag, Cologne, 1998

Knaack, U., Führer, W., Wurm, J.: Konstruktiver Glasbau 2. Neue Möglichkeiten und Techniken. Rudolf Müller Verlag, Cologne, 2000

Kohlmaier, G., v. Sartory, B.: Houses of Glass. A Nineteenth-Century Building Type. The MIT Press, Cambridge Massachusetts, 1990

Krewinkel, H.: Glass Buildings. Material, Structure and Detail. Birkhäuser, Basel, 1998

Lam, W. M. C.: Perception and lighting as formgivers for architecture. McGraw-Hill Inc., 1977 Baden-Württemberg Building Technology Office: Überkopfverglasungen im Rahmen von Zustimmungen im Einzelfall. Memorandum G1; ed. of 15 Apr 2008. Tübingen regional authority, 2008

Löffler, V., Kutzer, C.: Bauaufsichtliche Regelung bei der Verwendung/Anwendung von ungeregelten Bauprodukten bzw. Bauarten im Einzelfall nach Sächsischer Bauordnung. In: Weller, B. (ed.): glasbau2004; Proceedings. Institute of Building Construction, Technische Universität Dresden, Dresden 2004, pp. 19–37

Loudon, J. C.: An Encyclopaedia Of Cottage, Farm,

And Villa Architecture, And Furniture... Longman, Rees, Orme, Brown, Green, & Longman et al., London, 1833

Luible, A.: Stabilität von Tragelementen aus Glas. Dissertation. Ecole Polytechnique Fédérale de Lausanne, 2004

McKean, J.: Joseph Paxton. Crystal Palace. London, 1851. In: McKean, J., Parissien, S., Durant, S.: Lost Masterpieces. Joseph Paxton, Crystal Palace; Ferdinand Dutert, Palais Des Machines; McKim, Mead and White, Pennsylvania Station (Architecture 3s). Phaidon Press, London, 1999

Meyer, A. G.: Eisenbauten. Ihre Geschichte und Ästhetik; reprint of the Paul Neff Verlag ed., Esslingen, 1907. Gebrüder Mann Verlag, Berlin, 1997

Nijsse, R.: Glass in Structures: Elements, Concepts, Designs. Birkhäuser, Basel, 2003

O'Callaghan, J., Coult, G.: An all-glass cube in New York City. In: Glass Performance Days Tamglass Ltd. Oy: Glass Performance Days. 10th International Conference on Architectural and Automotive Glass. Glass Performance Days Ltd. Oy, Tampere, 2007, pp. 98–101

Petzold, A., Marusch, H., Schramm, B.: Der Baustoff Glas. Verlag für Bauwesen, Berlin, 1990

Pottgiesser, U.: Fassadenschichtungen – Glas. Mehrschalige Glaskonstruktionen. Typologie, Energie, Konstruktionen, Projektbeispiele. Bauwerk. Berlin, 2004

Rice, P., Dutton H.: Structural Glass, Routledge, 2001

Richards, B.: New Glass Architecture. Laurence King Publishing Ltd, London, 2006

Reidt, A.: Erläuterungen zur Leitlinie für die europäische technische Zulassung für geklebte Glaskonstruktionen. In: VDI (ed.): VDI report 1527. Bauen mit Glas. VDI Verlag GmbH, Düsseldorf, 2000, pp. 19–37

Reidt, A.: Allgemeine bauaufsichtliche Zulassungen im Glasbau. In: Weller, B. (ed.): glasbau2004; Proceedings, Institute of Building Construction, Technische Universität Dresden, Dresden, 2004, pp. 7–18

Reidt, A.: Europäische Technische Zulassungen. In: Weller, B. (ed.): glasbau2005; Proceedings, Institute of Building Construction, Technische Universität Dresden, Dresden 2005, pp. 5–22

Rowe, C., Slutzky, R.: Transparency; 3rd ed., Birkhäuser, Basel, 2009

Schadow, T.: Beanspruchungsgerechtes Konstruieren von Klebverbindungen in Glastragwerken. Dissertation. Building Design Institute, Technische Universität Dresden, Dresden, 2006

Schittich, C. et al.: Glass Construction Manual; 2nd ed., Institut für Internationale Architektur-Dokumentation, Munich, 2006

Sedlacek, G., Blank, K., Laufs, W., Güsgen, J.: Glas im Konstruktiven Ingenieurbau. Ernst & Sohn, Berlin, 1999

Schneider, J., Siegele K.: Glasecken. Konstruktion, Gestaltung, Beispiele. Deutsche Verlags-Anstalt, Munich, 2005

Schreiner, H., Nordhues, H.-W.: Fassaden; In: Bergmeister, K., Wörner, J.-D.: BetonKalender 2003. Hochhäuser und Geschossbauten. Ernst & Sohn, Berlin, 2003, pp. 207–302

Siebert, G.: Entwurf und Bemessung von tragenden Bauteilen aus Glas. Ernst & Sohn, Berlin, 2001

Siebert, G., Herrmann, T., Haese, A.: Konstruktiver Glasbau. Grundlagen und Bemessung. In: Kuhlmann, U. (ed.): Stahlbaukalender 2007; Ernst & Sohn, Berlin, 2007, chap. 7, pp. 499–568

Stark, J., Wicht, B.: Geschichte der Baustoffe. In: Schriften der Hochschule für Architektur und Bauwesen Weimar No. 99. Faculty of Civil Engineering, Chair of Building Materials, Weimar, 1995, pp. 151–164

Tasche, S.: Strahlungshärtende Acrylate im Konstruktiven Glasbau. Dissertation. Institute of Building Construction, Technische Universität Dresden, Dresden, 2008

Timm, G.: Bautechnische Prüfung und Überwachung der Bauausführung von Glaskonstruktionen. In: VDI (ed.): VDI report 1527. Bauen mit Glas; VDI Verlag GmbH, Düsseldorf, 2000, pp. 235–243

VDMA, Messe Düsseldorf GmbH (ed.): GLAS(S). Edition II. Woeste, Essen, 2002

Wachsmann, K.: Wendepunkt im Bauen. Krausskopf-Verlag, Wiesbaden, 1959

Weller, B., Nicklisch, F., Thieme, S., Weimar, T.: Glasbau Praxis. Konstruktion, Berechnung, Ausführung. Bauwerk, Berlin 2009

Weller, B.; Pottgiesser, U.; Tasche, S.: Adhesive Fixing in Building – Glass Construction; Part 1: Applications. In: Detail, Oct 2004, pp. 1166–1170

Weller, B.; Pottgiesser, U.; Tasche, S.: Adhesive Fixing in Building – Glass Construction; Part 2: Principles. In: Detail, Dec 2004, pp. 1488–1494

Weller, B.; Reich, S.; Wünsch, J.: Glasbau. In: Wendehorst Beispiele aus der Baupraxis. Pub. by O. W. Wetzell. B. G. Teubner, Stuttgart/Leipzig/Wiesbaden, 2007, pp. 211–241

Weller, B.; Tasche, S.; Weimar, T.: Glasbau. In: Holschemacher, K. (ed.): Entwurfs- und Berechnungstafeln für Architekten; Bauwerk-Verlag, Berlin, 2007, pp. 2.83–2.112

Weller, B.; Härth, K., Wünsch, J.: Regelwerke, Prüfungen und Überwachungen im Konstruktiven Glasbau. In: Der Prüfingenieur; No. 31. Berlin, 2007, pp. 127–137

Weller, B., Reich, S., Ebert, J., Krampe, P.: Individual approval of a vault with in-plane loaded glass panes. In: Glass Performance Days Glaston Finland Oy: Glass Performance Days. 11th International Conference on Architectural and Automotive Glass. Glass Performance Days Glaston Finland Oy, Tampere 2009, pp. 398–402

Weller, B.; Tasche, S.: Glasbau. In: Wetzell, O. W.: Wendehorst Bautechnische Zahlentafeln; B. G. Teubner, Stuttgart/Leipzig/Wiesbaden, 2007, pp. 883–914

Wigginton, M.: Glass in Architecture. Phaidon Press, London, 1996

Weller, B., Weimar, T., Krampe, P., Walther, A.: Glass-Steel Beams. Development of Hybrid Structures. GlassPerformance Days Glaston Finland Oy: Glass Performance Days. 11th International Conference on Architectural and Automotive Glass. Glass Performance Days Glaston Finland Oy, Tampere 2009, pp. 435–439

Wörner, J.-D., Schneider, J., Fink, A.: Glasbau. Grundlagen, Berechnung, Konstruktion. Springer-Verlag, Berlin, 2001

Wörner, J.-D., Schneider, J.: DIN 18008 – Glas im Bauwesen. Bemessungs- und Konstruktionsregeln. Stahlbau Spezial – Konstruktiver Glasbau. Ernst & Sohn, Berlin, 2008, pp. 3–9

Woods, M., Warren, A.: Glass Houses. A History of Greenhouses, Orangeries and Conservatories. Rizzoli International Publications, Inc., 1988

Wurm, J.: Gläserne Spannweiten. Strukturformen von Dachtragwerken aus Flachglas. Dissertation. Aachen, 2005

Wurm, J.: Glass Structures: Design and Construction of Self-supporting Skins. Birkhäuser, Basel, 2007

Manufacturers, companies and trade associations (selection)

Bauglasindustrie GmbH (Pilkington)
www.pilkington.de

BGT Bischoff Glastechnik AG
www.bgt-bretten.de

BLUHM & PLATE
www.bluhm.de

COLT
www.coltinfo.co.uk

DELO Industrie Klebstoffe
www.delo.de

DORMA
www.dorma-uk.co.uk

Dow Corning
www.dowcorning.com

Eckelt Glas GmbH
www.eckelt.at

F.A. Firman Ltd.
www.firmanglass.com

Flachglas MarkenKreis GmbH
www.flachglas-markenkreis.de

Frener + Reifer Metallbau GmbH
www.frener-reifer.com

Josef Gartner GmbH
www.josef-gartner.de

Glas Marte GmbH & Co KG
www.glasmarte.at

Glasbau Hahn GmbH & Co. KG
www.glasbau-hahn.de

Glasid AG
www.glasid.com

Glaswerke Arnold GmbH + Co. KG
www.glaswerke-arnold.de

Guardian Europe S.a r.l.
www.guardian-europe.com

Hunsrücker Glasveredelung Wagener GmbH & Co. KG
www.glaswagener.de

INGLAS
www.inglas.de

Inoutic / Deceuninck GmbH
www.inoutic.com

INTERPANE GLAS INDUSTRIE AG
www.interpane.de

KL-megla GmbH
www.kl-megla.de

Mayer'sche Hofkunstanstalt
www.mayersche-hofkunst.de

Mermet S.A.
www.sunscreen-mermet.com

Mero – TSK International GmbH & Co. KG
www.mero.de

M-Systems
www.m-systems.at

OKALUX GmbH
www.okalux.de

Pilkington Group Ltd.
www.pilkington.com

Roschmann Konstruktionen
www.roschmann.de

Rosenheimer Glastechnik GmbH
www.rosenheimer-glastechnik.de

SAINT-GOBAIN Glass
www.saint-gobain-glass.com

Sanco Beratung
www.sanco.de

Schindler GmbH & Co. KG
www.schindler-roding.de

Schmidlin Ltd.
www.lindner-schmidlin.com

Schollglas Holding- u. Geschäftsführungs GmbH
www.schollglas.com

SCHOTT AG
www.schott.com

Schüco International KG
www.schueco.de

Ernst Schweizer AG Metallbau
www.schweizer-metallbau.ch

SEKISUI S-LEC BV
www.s-lec.nl

Semcoglas Holding GmbH
www.semcoglas.com

Sika Ltd.
www.sika.co.uk

Solaris Glasbausteine
www.sevesglassblock.com

Tambest Oy
www.tambest.fi/en

Technical Glass Products
www.tgpamerica.com/surfacing/neoparies

Thiele AG
www.thiele-ag.de

Tremco illbruck GmbH & Co. KG
www.tremco-illbruck.com

Tuchschmid Constructa AG
www.tuchschmid.ch

Index

Picture credits

The authors and publishers would like to express their sincere gratitude to all those who have assisted in the production of this book, be it through providing photos or artwork or granting permission to reproduce their documents or providing other information. All the drawings in this book were specially commissioned. Photographs not specifically credited were taken by the architects or are works photographs or were supplied from the archives of the magazine DETAIL. Despite intensive endeavours we were unable to establish copyright ownership in just a few cases; however, copyright is assured. Please notify us accordingly in such instances.

page 8:
Giles Breton, London

page 9 left:
Michael Wurzbach, Hamburg

page 9 centre:
ZSW, Stuttgart

page 9 right, 16 centre, 19 right,
42 bottom, 101 bottom:
Christian Schittich, Munich

page 13 right, 15 right, 24 left, 38 right, 40 right,
50 left, 62, 63, 64, 67, 70, 71 right, 81:
Stefan Unnewehr, Dresden

page 15 left, 68:
Jan Wurm, London

page 16 left:
Angelo Kaunat, Bürmoos (A)

page 16 right:
Margherita Spiluttini, Vienna

page 17:
Nigel Young/Foster + Partners, London

page 18:
Lothar Sprenger, Dresden

page 19 left:
Schott AG, Grünenplan

page 24 right:
Tübingen regional authority, Ulm Firearms Office

page 25:
Fraunhofer Institute for High-Speed Dynamics,
Ernst Mach Institute, Freiburg

page 28:
Schott Jenaer Glas GmbH

page 34:
H. G. Esch, Hennef

page 35:
Nigel Young, London

page 37:
Jörg Schöner, Dresden

page 40 left, 49 top right:
Octatube, Delft

page 42 top:
Luuk Kramer, Amsterdam

page 42 centre:
Luke Lowings, London

page 43 left:
Marios C. Phocas, Nicosia

page 43 right:
HI-TEC-GLAS GmbH, Grünenplan

page 44 top, 101 top right:
Christian Richters/artur, Essen

page 44 centre:
Bernhard Kroll, Grosshansdorf

page 44 bottom, 51 top left, 51 bottom:
seele, GSSG Holding GmbH & Co. KG, Gersthofen

page 45:
Frank Oudeman, New York

page 46:
GOP Architekten, Münster

page 49 top left:
Hans-Chistian Schink, Leipzig

page 49 bottom:
Gabriela Metzger, Stuttgart

page 50:
Maier-Glas GmbH, Heidenheim

page 51 top right:
Heinz W. Krewinkel, Böblingen

page 52, 54 centre:
Courtesy of Apple

page 53:
Hufton+Crow/View/artur, Essen

page 54 bottom:
Ed Reeve, London

page 55:
Isolar-Glas-Beratung GmbH, Kirchberg

page 76:
Martin Romstedt, Schwäbisch Hall

page 78:
Gerhard Hagen, Bamberg

page 79 left:
Saint Gobain, Aachen

page 80 left, centre:
Stefan Reich, Dresden

page 80 right:
Ulrich van Stipriaan, Dresden

page 84, 85:
Courtesy of Andy Ryan/Nelson Atkins Museum
of Art, 2007

page 86, 87:
Olaf Mahlstedt/archenova, Düsseldorf

page 88, 89:
Roger Frei, Zurich

page 91, 92:
Florian Holzherr, Munich

page 93, 94, 101 bottom left:
Christian Richters, Münster

page 95, 96:
Werner Huthmacher/artur, Essen

page 98, 99 right:
Antoine Duhamel, Paris

page 99 left:
Yves Chanoit, Paris

page 100:
José Hevia, Barcelona

Full-page plates

page 6:
Kibble Palace (Crystal Palace), Glasgow (GB), 1872,
John Kibble, Graeme Phanco, Duntocher (GB)

page 10:
Hearst Tower, New York City, New York (USA), 2006,
Foster + Partners, James Carpenter Design Associates,
Andreas Keller/artur, Essen

page 20:
Facade of IAC Building, New York City, New York (USA),
2007, Frank O. Gehry, Dominique Roski, New York

page 32:
Klein Residence, Santa Fe, New Mexico (USA), 2004,
Ohlhausen, DuBois Architects, Frank Oudeman,
New York

page 56:
Musée d'Art, Strasbourg (F), 1996, Adrien Fainsilber,
seele, GSSG Holding GmbH & Co. KG, Gersthofen

page 72:
glasstec 2006, seele, GSSG Holding GmbH & Co. KG,
Gersthofen

page 82:
Memorial for the victims of the terrorist attacks of
11 March 2004, Madrid (E), 2007, Estudio FAM,
Esaú Acosta Pérez, Madrid

page 102:
Federal State Central Bank, Meiningen, 2000, Hans
Kohlhoff and Helga Zimmermann, Schott AG, Mainz

The authors and publishers would like to thank the trade organisation Fachverband Konstruktiver Glasbau e.V. for their generous assistance with this publication.